NARRATIVE DESIGN FOR WRITERS

EDWIN MCRAE

FICTION ENGINE

INTRODUCTION_

There's *never* been a better time to be a writer in the games industry.

For writers, the games industry is a *much* more welcoming and understanding place than it was ten years ago, when I first started on this crazy, winding path. It took a while, but story is now universally accepted as a vital part of the game development process. Well, almost. No, not all games need a plot, but even your most basic Match 3 mobile game benefits massively from having a story context. As Lisa Cron said, we humans are "wired for story". It's how we make sense of the world, and it's how we make sense of our video games.

Play is what we do. Story is why we do it.

It's also a much bigger industry, meaning there are so many more games in need of stories and writing. You're tapping into an industry worth over $120 billion dollars in 2019.

Mobile games make up over 50% of the industry and, in 2019, free-to-play (F2P) games out-earned premium games (including the big AAA titles like Red Dead Redemption 2 and Assassin's Creed Odyssey) by four to one. That's *particularly* good news for you, dear writer, because F2P games are content hungry beasts that frequently need story and scripts for expansions and events.

Not to mention that the sheer variety of games is legion. If you're a freelancer, or maybe a staff writer working for a mobile games company, you could write up a world doc for a squad tactics game in the morning, produce flavor text for their cute collectable monsters game after lunch, and write NPC interactive dialogue until the end of business that day. Then tomorrow might be completely different again!

Sound exciting? Good! It really can be.

But there's a trick to being a writer in the games industry.

Creative versatility.

Because one game can be *so* different from another, a narrative designer needs to adapt to many styles and storytelling techniques. Sorry, it's not enough to be an accomplished novelist or scriptwriter or poet or comic book storyliner or website copywriter. On any day, you might be asked to apply skills from *all* of those disciplines.

And then there's the player to contend with. With linear art forms like TV and novels, you can craft a sophisticated plot knowing that you are in *complete control* of the story. The audience won't jump out of their seats, reach through the screen, pen in hand, and scribble an alternate ending across your beautifully crafted climax. In games, the audience will do exactly that. They'll scribble across your entire script if you let them! In fact we, as game developers, expect them to.

So how do you be a scriptwriting, storylining, poetic, copywriting novelist to an audience that just won't sit still?

That's what this book is about.

I'll take you through the principles of narrative design and show you a few tried-and-true techniques I've learned and developed through my years of writing for video games.

But most importantly, I'll show you the mindset a narrative

designer needs to create a sustainable career for themselves in the games industry. I *don't* mean the usual combination of positive affirmations and workaholism. I'm talking about the actual thought processes you need to be engaging in to *train your brain*. Narrative design is like nothing else I've encountered. It requires some unique neural wiring to hold an entire game concept in your mind, story and mechanics included.

That's why it's important to engage in the right thought and design processes *now*. Neural plasticity is amazing. Your brain can rewire surprisingly quickly. But it's not an overnight thing. It takes time and practice.

So let's get started!

FROM WRITER TO NARRATIVE DESIGNER_

> ARE YOU A GAME WRITER OR A NARRATIVE DESIGNER?

> HOW IS WRITING FOR GAMES DIFFERENT FROM NON-INTERACTIVE
MEDIUMS?

> SHOULD STORY SERVE MECHANICS OR VICE VERSA?

WHAT'S THE DIFFERENCE BETWEEN GAME WRITING AND NARRATIVE DESIGN?_

A game writer produces all the narrative bits that a player will see and hear within the game. Dialogues, flavor texts, diaries... basically any kind of in-game text or voice over.

A narrative designer does the higher level stuff like storylines, world building, lore development, character creation... all the background material that forges a story context for the player. And it's the ND's (narrative designer's) job to make sure the story works with and enhances the gameplay. NDs are there to design a story-rich player experience, these days often dealing with procedural systems and designing for emergent narrative. Game writers are there to bring the ND's design to life through dialogue and in-game text.

Can you do both? Yes, and that's often the case, especially in the Indie video game sector. Being a freelance narrative designer *and* game writer, I will often see a game through right from the world-building to NPC dialogue. In fact, that's exactly what I've been doing for Project Haven, an Indie cyberpunk turn-based tactical RPG.

As of writing this, I've worked with the Foresight Games founders over the last four years, helping them to:

1. build their cyberpunk city
2. create and flesh out their player characters (PCs) and non-player characters (NPCs)
3. storyline a 5-act narrative arc
4. come up with missions that the player must complete to progress through the narrative arc
5. write the dialogue and in-game text for the missions, and flavorful moments between missions to help deepen the world and characters.

Steps 1 to 4 would usually fall under the 'narrative designer' mantle. Step 5 is definitely game writer territory.

But it's all writing.

You see, the challenge of defining 'writing for games' is the same challenge we have when defining what a 'video game' even is. If we're talking about a linear story-driven game like Deus Ex: Human Revolution or Tomb Raider, then there's not much difference at all. Three Act structure, Hero's Journey and all those other writing techniques still apply.

But if you're writing for a procedural RPG like Darkest Dungeon or a city builder like Goblins of Elderstone, then it couldn't be more different. Instead of writing a 'story', you're writing a whole collection of tiny narrative bits (narbs - see Chapter Eleven) that add up to a story only once the player encounters them in the game. And that player might encounter those narbs in any order, possible missing whole swathes of them in the process. Any concept of plot goes out the window. That's when narrative design becomes more closely related to theme park design or interior design than to writing films or novels. You're creating an experience to enjoy, not a plot to follow.

With film, TV and books, we're used to *following* a main character. It's a vicarious experience. We tag along on their journey. With games, the player *is* the main character. Video games have changed the way we relate to a story by giving us agency. And creating interesting and rewarding journeys for players, that's what I think is special about narrative design.

Narrative design is about using Story to ensure that Play has Meaning.

And because narrative design focuses on enhancing gameplay, actions must speak louder than words.

The player isn't there to read or listen.

The player is there to play.

So a narrative designer must learn to think in actions, first and foremost. Rather than telling the player a story, we are asking a player to take certain actions so they will come to understand the story through play. The ND's job is to add the story context, the name of the monster, how they became a monster, why they need to be defeated, what the player will gain from the Win in story terms. Level Designers create Bosses and Loot Drops. Narrative Designers create Villains and Emotional Payoffs.

It's up to a narrative designer to describe the story experience (see Chapter Two) the player will have to convey it to the game designer through documents and diagrams so they can integrate mechanics and story into a fun and fulfilling game.

Yes, narrative designers can help to create the fundamental game concept before the first line of code is even written.

Once upon a time, 'writers' came in near the end of the game to create dialogue and supply in-game text. That was the only time game devs allowed someone with a writer brain near the project. Alas, in those dark ages the story was a bit of an afterthought. A cherry on top. One of those cheap, artificially colored and flavored cherries.

Thankfully, that's changed a great deal over the last ten years.

Narrative designers are often there at the beginning of the process to ensure that story and gameplay walk hand in hand from premise to production. More and more, NDs can evolve game premises like 'kill a horde of monsters, collect a ton of loot and save the princess' into 'survive, grow as a character and experience a meaningful relationship'.

The character arcs of Booker and Elizabeth in Bioshock Infinite exemplify this, as does the relationship that forms between them. We've come a long way since Donkey Kong.

The question is: where to next?

That's for the ND to work out with the player.

CREATING A STORY EXPERIENCE_

In many respects, a narrative designer is a hybrid of writer and user-experience (UX) designer. UX designers study player behavior and tweak everything from gameplay and UI to art and marketing in an effect to create the most satisfying and enjoyable experience possible for the player.

A narrative design does pretty much the same thing, but through the lense of story. It's the ND's job to forge the 'story experience' of a game.

> WHAT DO I MEAN BY 'STORY EXPERIENCE'?

Let's go back to my earlier comparison of narrative design with theme park design. Take a classic Ghost Train, for instance. As a narrative designer, you have to sit yourself down in that imaginary, rattling ghost train and think about how you are going to both engage and scare the bejesus out of the passenger.

What style of horror are you going for?

- B-grade retro?
- Psychological thriller?
- Splatter and gore?
- Alien invasion?
- Creeping Lovecraftian dread?

What fears do you want to play on?

- Fear of death?
- Fear of sickness?
- Claustrophobia?
- Fear of the unknown?
- Fear of being a puppet?
- Fear of insanity?

And once that's all decided, you have to think up the monsters, the settings, the emotional journey and everything else that goes into an awesomely scary theme park ride. And that's before you've even written a single line of prose or dialogue!

In this way, being a narrative designer differs greatly from being a scriptwriter for television or a novelist. You don't create a full draft of your work and then present it to the director or editor. Narrative design is an ongoing conversation with the development team as you work together to create both a mentally satisfying 'play' experience and an emotionally satisfying 'story' experience.

And this sort of experience design starts right at the beginning of development... with World Building.

Where? When? Why is the world this way? Characters and creatures aren't set in an environment. Characters and creatures grow from an environment.

With sci-fi and fantasy worlds, everything needs to be decided. Climates. Cultures. Catastrophes... and a whole swag of other elements starting with 'C', and a few other letters too. Even with strictly historical or contemporary environments, the 'Where', 'When' and 'Why' still need careful selection from the contexts available.

A narrative designer's job is to answer questions before the player can even ask them.

1066, England

- The Norman invasion or the Norwegian invasion?
- Why did the Normans win?
- Why did the Norwegians lose?
- Why were there two seemingly unconnected armies invading within days of each other?
- Why was anybody invading at all?

My previous book, Narrative Design for Indies, has a whole chapter on world building so I won't go into the nitty-gritty of it here. Suffice to say that it's the ND's job to make sure the players are asking questions like "Who is that mysterious Norman knight who just saved my armored butt?" versus "Why does this world feel like an amateur LARPing weekend?"

ND is about creating a world that a player can temporarily believe in. It's different from a TV character who inherently believes in their own fictional world. Jon Snow isn't aware that he's part of a fantasy television show, even though Kit Harrington is.

In fact, the player is very much like an actor coming into a role. The richer the fictional world you offer them, the easier it is for the actor to immerse themselves in that role and produce a convincing performance. But if they're constantly having to ask questions and point out holes in the fourth wall, they're not going to enjoy the experience and their performance will suffer for it.

And it's not just the surroundings that need to be believable. The player's actions must be believable too. Unlike a novel character who will do what the writer tells them to, a player must have agency. They must have a reasonable level of freedom within the confines of the game mechanics, and the game world needs to acknowledge that freedom.

For instance...

The 'Eye for an Eye Quest' is considered completed once the player has killed the Cyclops and delivered its Eye to Anthea of Wytchery.

- What will Anthea say if the player returns while the Cyclops is still alive?
- What if the player has killed the Cyclops but not collected the Eye?
- What if the player kills the Cyclops before receiving the quest brief from Anthea?
- What if the player kills the Cyclops and delivers the Eye before receiving the quest brief from Anthea?

That's a relatively common and simple RPG example. Imagine how much more complicated it could get if there were three different cyclops, three different body parts on order, and a rival witch NPC who also wants those parts.

The ND should think through every permutation of an in-game situation and ensure that the story recognizes the player's choices.

Yes, that's a fundamental mindset shift that I had to make when I moved from TV scriptwriting over to game writing, and later... narrative design. I had to get my head around the fact that there wasn't just one plot going on here. I wasn't dealing with a single story arc. I was having to take a complete 360 degree view of the story. That requires some hard-core visualization, and it takes time for those neural pathways to grow and develop.

Yes, there were headaches. But neural plasticity is a truly wondrous thing, and it's amazing how quickly your mind can expand to encompass multiple realities all existing at the same time.

It just takes practice.

GAME MECHANICS_

So if story experience is a combination of narrative and mechanics, how do *you* feel about the relationship between those two vital game elements?

1. Should the story serve the mechanics?
2. Should mechanics serve the story?

> 2. STORY-DRIVEN GAMES

If you answered '2' then the good news is that there are many game developers out there making those kinds of games. These are proper 'story-driven' games where the mechanics are there to support the storytelling.

Guardian Māia is an example of one such game that I've written. It's a mobile text adventure game where you guide a Māori warrior woman through a blend of mythical and post-apocalyptic Aotearoa. The main UI is multiple choice. I wrote it in Inkle's Ink Script to track choices, and the text can change based on the actions the player chooses for Māia. There's also a story-driven combat system where the player selects combat moves based on what they've read and intuited from the written description of their opponent. It was the combat system in the Way of the Tiger gamebook series, written by Mark Smith and Jamie Thomson, that served as inspiration for the combat system in Guardian Māia. In those books you are a ninja and can select various martial arts moves to try against your opponents. Turn to 111 to unleash a Forked Lightning Kick. Turn to 325 to unleash a Dragon's Tail Throw. I played those gamebooks when I was a tween back in the late 80s and the experience really stuck with me, so I set out to recreate that story-driven combat experience in Guardian Māia.

Telltale games are another great example of this. They've created interactive story versions of The Walking Dead, Game of Thrones and The Wolf Among Us (from the Fable comics.) And it takes a real narrative designer's brain to develop the multitude of choices and consequences available in those games. There's also Tin Man who create digital adventure gamebooks, many of which are remakes of or based on the original Fighting Fantasy gamebooks by Ian Livingstone and Steve Jackson. There's also Inkle, creators of 80 Days and the Sorcery! remakes, Cubus who created Frankenstein Wars, Choice of Games, and a host of interactive story platforms like Episodes and Choices who are targeting younger and casual interactive fiction markets.

If interactive fiction appeals to you, then there's work to be had out there, or you can publish your own interactive fiction through various channels. As of writing, Choice of Games is probably the most established avenue there, and Tales: Choose your own story is a promising new arrival on the scene.

As mentioned before, regarding Guardian Māia, I used Inkle's Ink Script, which is an open source scripting language that plays nicely with Unity. There's a thriving Ink Script community, and if you know your way around Unity, or can team up with a Unity developer, then you can create some sophisticated interactive fiction.

And if text adventures aren't your thing, then there are plenty of developers out there making linear, story-driven gaming experiences. To my mind, the best example is Frictional Games who made Amnesia: Dark Descent and SOMA. I would go as far as to call these games 'interactive movies' where the game mechanics are relatively simple and they focus the experience on exploration of the world and discovery of the overarching plot. Alan Wake is another excellent example of this, and the makers, Remedy Entertainment, depict themselves as creators of 'cinematic blockbusters'. And let's not forget the most recent Tomb Raider games.

So there's plenty of work out there for narrative designers with a story-driven focus, but story-driven games are definitely in the minority. I don't want to put you off though. Story-driven games can be both deeply satisfying to create and financially viable to work on. I'll be diving more into the story-driven side of things later in this book, and there are plenty of techniques from the 'mechanically driven' side of game development, which I'll also cover later in this book, that can enrich a story-driven gaming experience.

> 1. MECHANICALLY DRIVEN GAMES

If you chose '1' then I can give you even better news. The vast majority of narrative design gigs are yours for the taking! Speaking from experience here, mechanics are 'king' in the world of game development. Play comes first and story comes second. You can have a great game that doesn't contain a scrap of intentionally written story, but a story without play is simply a story. It's not even a bad game... it's just not a game.

When approaching narrative design, mindset is the most important factor. It takes a classic writer brain quite some time to adjust to the unique demands of narrative design. I've been through that rather painful process myself. You can honestly feel your grey matter rewiring and it's not always a comfortable experience.

But if you're a gamer, your brain is already part way there. If you've been a game master for tabletop roleplaying, you're another step closer. Add in some copywriting and UX experience and you're getting even closer. But it's ok if you don't have any of that latter experience. If, for instance, you're a science fiction, fantasy or horror writer who has been playing games most of your life, you're off to a great start.

This is because you already instinctively understand what a 'story experience' is. You've been experiencing them for yourself. Rather than reading about the trials and tribulations of this or that protagonist, you've been that protagonist.

The most important thing to remember with mechanically driven games is that the player is in the driving seat. You can lead a player to a story but you can't make them read. If they want to skip your carefully crafted cut scene, burn your lovingly written lore tomes or spend their entire in-game time on daily quests and grinding, they can. It's their show.

So our challenge, as narrative designers, is to have our players absorb story without even noticing. Rather than telling them a story, we enrich their play experience with story. Yes, the story experience strikes again.

I'll be offering plenty of tips on how to create an effective story experience later in the book, especially when we look at Part 4 - Narrative Design Processes.

In the meantime, here's a joke for you. What do you get when you cross a gamer with a writer?

PREPARING FOR YOUR NARRATIVE DESIGN CAREER_

> IS YOUR STORY BRAIN TUNED IN?

> ARE YOUR WRITING SKILLS SHARP?

> ARE YOU READY TO RUN A BUSINESS?

WHAT DO YOU GET WHEN YOU CROSS A GAMER WITH A WRITER?_

Not a comedian.

> ONE NARRATIVE DESIGNER'S JOURNEY

Let's get the "me me me" bit out of the way. Yes, I'm an example of someone who has taken a circuitous route to becoming a narrative designer. Yes, there are some clues in my journey that might help you. I'd really rather talk about the topic than about myself, but people keep asking me how I became a narrative designer, so... here it is, quick and hopefully painless.

> THE 80S

I played A LOT of video games, starting when my family got an Atari 600XL for Christmas when I was about ten. And I wrote A LOT of stories for my entertainment and the very patient amusement of my parents. Mostly fantasy and science-fiction.

> THE 90S

That continued until I went to university in the early 90s where, because of all the bloody essays I had to write, I gave up on writing... but not on gaming. I was supposed to be getting a degree in English Literature, Film Studies and Psychology, but I spent far more time studying Diablo, Starcraft, Civilization and Privateer 2. Near the end of uni, I had a bit of a meltdown, dropped out of my Masters in Psychology and started writing again. That said, I didn't completely drop out. I had two post-grad film papers I was still trucking on with, particularly a mini-thesis on 'The representation of Virtual Reality in Film'. See? Obsessed with game worlds. I just hadn't realised it yet.

Right, things to note so far.

1. LOTS of writing.
2. LOTS of gaming.
3. A tenuous grip on reality and the accepted priorities of a 'normal life'.
4. Obsessed with virtual worlds.
5. A crisis where I dropped out of the 'sensible' career pathway.

In the late 90s, you'd think I would've realised that video games were my thing, but video game writing still wasn't a recognizable career and the internet was still so primitive that I would've had to move from New Zealand to the US to even get a look in. At least, that's what I believed. So what did I do instead? I launched into the first of many 'shadow careers'.

This is what writer and creative self-help guru, Steven Pressfield, says about shadow careers.

Sometimes, when we're terrified of embracing our true calling, we'll pursue a shadow calling instead. That shadow career is a metaphor for our real career. Its shape is similar, its contours feel tantalizingly the same."

> THE 00S

Being a farm boy from rural Southland, I was far too scared to shift to the US to 'embrace my true calling' so I trained for a year and got a job in my first shadow career. Teaching. Yup, I became a high school drama teacher thanks to all of that am-dram I'd squeezed in around gaming during my high school years. I continued gaming, completing the Diablo expansion, Return to Castle Wolfenstein, Resident Evil 1 & 2, Silent Hill and Dynasty Warriors 4, just to name a few highlights.

I also continued with the writing, producing a whole swag of science fiction short stories that weren't half bad thanks to my being part of an online writing group that critiqued the living crap out of my work. After publishing about a dozen short stories in online e-zines and getting my first taste of earning money from writing (a whole five Canadian dollars for one story!), I set to the gargantuan task of writing a cyberpunk novel. I was quite the fan of William Gibson, Jeff Noon and The Matrix, you see. Well, that novel never got published, and during a brief stint in the UK, my attempts to get into the TV industry crashed and burned. I carried on teaching drama until I had another wake-up call after writing and directing a cyberpunk musical in 2005.

Shadow career number two. Writing and producing musicals.

Burned out and utterly sick of teaching, because it wasn't really what I wanted to be doing anyway, I took a chance and used the musical script to apply for the Masters in Scriptwriting at Victoria University of Wellington. *And then one day... I got in.*

More things to note:

1. I practiced short-form storytelling and got good enough to get published on a small scale.
2. Drama teaching helped hone my storytelling skills.
3. I had to hit a crisis point to take any big leaps of faith.
4. By writing and producing my own stuff, I got noticed.
5. Through thick and thin, I kept gaming.
6. I thought the world wasn't ready yet for me to tackle game writing. In hindsight, it was just me not being ready.

Onwards to 2006, where I tried my hand at film scriptwriting and ended up creating a thinly veiled kids adventure game.

Shadow career three. Film script writer.

During that year, while I completed my masters and worked full time as a teacher and uni tutor (!!), I got a work placement at South Pacific Pictures on New Zealand's major TV soap opera, Shortland Street. The work placement turned into a writing tryout, which turned into a full-time storylining gig.

Shadow career four. TV storyliner and scriptwriter.

I did that for four straight years, learning how to write fast, wrangle lots of different characters and storylines, and probably the most important lesson of all, not to be precious about my writing. If ever there's a 'school of hard knocks' for writers, it's the TV industry, especially serial drama. Still, it wasn't all bad.

Like I said, I learned heaps, and I got to create a serial killer and a mad scientist... and choreograph an Indian wedding, which was fun. But the scariest thing about this time was how much less gaming I did. I think I completed House of the Dead: Overkill on the Wii and Speedball on the iPad. And that was it. I remember at one point vowing that I'd work in TV until I retired, and then I'd spend the rest of my days playing video games.

> THE 10S

Then it occurred to me. Why am I waiting until my 'dying years' to play video games? What happened to this thing that had grown to be a core aspect of my sense of self? I kinda wish I'd had that realization earlier, because it was around 2010 that this realization happened. But the New Zealand games industry still wasn't ready, and after my failures in England, I wasn't keen to try my luck overseas again. So I started playing more games, and blogged about games, while still soldiering on with soap opera writing.

Shadow career five. Blogger.

Then, as often happens, 'life' took a hand and gave me a solid shove off a cliff.

But before we get into that, let's check in on those points again.

1. Apart from getting that work placement at Shortland Street, the masters was a waste of time and money.
2. Writing for TV can suck the creative juice out of you, leaving little remaining for your own work.
3. Writing for TV taught me a lot of writing skills, super fast, and paid me to practice storytelling full time.

4. Even if you are writing fiction professionally, you can still blog in your passion area.

I got fired from South Pacific Pictures. After a promising start, I now seemed to struggle with expressing the 'Shortland Street voice', which wasn't surprising since I was absolutely hating it by this point. Sure, getting fired from my regular gig shook things up at home, and put me in a precarious financial situation, but it also gave me the kick in the butt I needed.

I scrambled about, got some professional blogging to pay the bills, barely, and went to the game developers meetups that had just started up in Auckland. This was 2010. And that's where I met the Grinding Gear Games guys and learned about Path of Exile. But that's getting ahead of myself. A game writing gig didn't eventuate until after I'd made a proof of concept for my game about a digital fairy trapped inside a mobile phone. This I did with a small team of game devs I'd met through the meetups, a photography student friend of mine, and an ex-Shortland Street actress. With a script, a game development document, and some in-game videos under my belt, plenty of blogging about games, and four years of TV-writing experience, I caught the attention of the Path of Exile team, got a message via Facebook saying they'd like to meet me, wrote an audition piece for them, and got the job.

Hooray! I'd made it! I was a game writer, at last. It washed away all of my worries. I'd found my Xanadu and I would live happily ever after.

Not quite.

1. I had to get fired from my cushy, hated job before I would put any effort into getting a game writing gig.
2. It was a combo of blogging, making my game, and

professional writing experience that got me my first
game writing job.
3. Mingling with game devs at meetups, that's what got
me on the right people's radar.

Path of Exile turned out to be a ten-hour per week gig. I now
had two kids, was renting a reasonably expensive house in Titi-
rangi (Auckland), and my professional blogging jobs were drying
up, fast. I went looking for some part-time high school teaching
work to pay the bills and got offered a full-time drama teaching
position at a pretty rough South Auckland school. Tired of 'hus-
tling' and scared of financial ruin, I took the teaching job and
squeezed the Path of Exile writing into free periods, evenings and
weekends.

Back to shadow career one.

It was an exhausting year, especially as the Path of Exile work
increased. I didn't get a lot of time for gaming, but I scratched that
itch a bit by introducing gaming into the classroom as a learning
tool. Educational games were popping up more and more, particularly 'serious' games, and these unruly South Auckland kids loved
anything that wasn't reading a book or writing essays. So it was a
win-win!

I survived 2011 through bloody-minded determination and
the fact that I loved writing for Path of Exile. Facing 2012, I still
didn't have enough hours to go full time as a game writer, but I
scored a part-time teaching gig in Nelson, so we upped sticks and
moved there so I could be a 50% game writer and 50% teacher. I
found short-term gigs on the mobile games Indie Music Manager
and Flutter to supplement the regular work with Path of Exile.
The music manager gig came through someone I'd met at the
Auckland game dev meetups, and the Flutter gig was from

someone I'd worked with at South Pacific Pictures who had also made the leap over to games.

And then I scored my first overseas game writing gigs. I learned a trick from somewhere. I can't remember where, but whoever came up with it was brilliant. This trick was the constructive criticism of games already out there in the market. For instance, the first time I did this was when I was approached by Blue Flame Publishing.

Blue Flame got in touch with me to ask for a review of their new digital gamebook they were working on called Hamnasya. They reached out to me because of my gaming blog. I played it, thought it was good, but found the writing long-winded. I said as much, in polite terms, and offered to edit the gamebook for them. I felt I was being cheeky, but figured it was worth a go. To my surprise, they thought it was a great idea and suddenly I had an entire gamebook to edit.

Something similar happened with Mechanist games in China. I played through the demo of City of Steam, saw a few things that could be improved in the delivery of the narrative, and got in touch with the creator via the website. It didn't lead immediately to a gig, but it led to a Skype meeting which led to a series of email discussions which led to meeting the creator again at GDC in San Francisco. That face-to-face finally led to me working on a new game that Mechanist were producing.

So there you go. A little constructive feedback can go a long way, but it has to be delivered very politely, and you have to be careful and astute with your analysis.

Where am I going with this? For me, networking and a half decent website showcasing my growing body of work enabled me to go full time with my game writing halfway through 2013. I said goodbye to my high school media studies class (shadow career number six), kept designing narratives and networking when needed, and that's been me ever since.

> NOW

I've laid this all out before you, not because I think it was the right way to get into a narrative design career, but to show you how one person did it. Basically, if I hadn't insisted on fleeing to half a dozen shadow careers along the way, I may have become a narrative designer of video games much, much sooner. Then again, it's very unwise to go back and try to change history, as Dr Who will readily tell you, so I'm happy to be where I am now and able to share the many years of game writing wisdom that I have accumulated.

I'm also convinced that my circuitous route into narrative design set me up with the skills and resilience to handle freelancing and working in the Indie gaming space. I've learned to be agile, react quickly to change, and to never put all my eggs in one basket. These days I feel more secure when I have a half dozen Indie or medium-sized game gigs on the go than I would if I had one full-time gig. I've been offered jobs like that. In-house. Full time. I've turned them down for two reasons.

1. I never want to rely on only one source of income again.
2. I find the Indie and mid-size gaming space much more creative and fulfilling than AAA.

But that's me. Let's get back to you.

LEARNING THE TROPES_

> FORMAL EDUCATION = A FORMALITY, REALLY

A little training never hurts. That, in my experience, has been true. However, a lot of training can hurt you a great deal. I'll see if I can explain what I mean by that.

On my journey, there were no stops along the way where I could learn at a tertiary institution. Not for narrative design, specifically. There was nothing online or offline that I could sink my teeth into, study for three years, and wave a certificate saying I've got a degree in narrative design at the end of it all.

> MAKE THE PRACTICAL CHOICE ABOUT LEARNING

Now there are plenty of courses around, but you really have to look at them closely to see what you will get out of it.

If the course has been designed by an industry professional, and better yet, if that industry professional will give you personal tutoring, then jump at the opportunity. If you think a Bachelors

Degree in Game Theory and Narrative Design Principles will get you a job in the video game industry, you might be disappointed.

Of course, I say this within the scope of my knowledge and experience. I'm focused on Indie game development and have been for most of my career. Perhaps it's a great idea to have a degree in narrative design theory if you want to get a gig with a AAA game dev company. I honestly don't know.

What I do know is that I've never been asked about my qualification in all my time writing for games. It's just not something that game devs seem all that interested in. Instead, they've always asked for descriptions of previous projects, samples of my work, and on rare occasions, they ask me to write an audition piece for them. I'll be talking about how to write a good audition piece or work sample later on in the book. In the meantime, let me just say that it seems to be more important to show narrative design experience, even if it's just interactive fiction that you've knocked up in your own time.

> GETTING IN

So here's how I think you can muscle your way into the Indie games industry.

Read, Play, Write

Read a lot of books.
Play a lot of games.
Write a lot of words.

> READ

First, read as many books as you can about narrative design. But only the ones written by narrative design professionals.

The good news for you–at the time of writing this book, there aren't that many books on narrative design. Barely enough to fill a bookshelf. So it won't take you too long to read them all.

And if you're still hungry for non-fiction after that, consider looking at gamer psychology books. The more you understand about gamers, and how they behave, the more effectively you'll be able to design narratives to satisfy and thrill them. Getting Gamers: The Psychology of Video Games by Jamie Madigan is an excellent place to start.

On the fiction front, read interaction fiction and gamelit/LitRPG.

For interactive fiction, I'd start with 80 Days by Inkle, The Frankenstein Wars by Cubus and Choice of Robots by Kevin Gold. These aren't simple pick-a-path stories. These are in-depth interactive experiences where the story genuinely responds to the reader's choices.

And for LitRPG, I'd recommend the Stonehaven League books by Carrie Summers and the Dungeon Lord series by Hugo Huesca. If you haven't come across LitRPG before, I'm not surprised. It's a relatively new genre with growing appeal. The stories are set inside virtual reality video games, and the game mechanics are obvious to the reader. They're an excellent insight into gamer psychology, particularly into what experiences gamers crave most from games and how invested one can become in the story context of a game. I've written three LitRPG novels, each with varying success. Warlock: Reign of Blood, Executioner: Reign of Blood and Skulls of Atlantis.

> PLAY

I can't state this one strongly enough. Play video games!

And I don't mean just story-driven games. Play widely, trying as many types of games as you can, but foremost, focus on the games that you always like to play.

Why? Simple, really. The games you enjoy are the ones you are ultimately best suited to write for. Narrative design is ultimately about combining storytelling with game mechanics. The better you understand and appreciate the game mechanics, the better you will work game mechanics and story into a symbiotic and satisfying experience.

It doesn't really matter if you like first-person shooters, real-time strategy games, point and click adventure games or immense MMORPGs. Every one of those genres tells the story in its own way, and it's only by experiencing those stories that you will start to spot the techniques of storytelling.

After each play session, jot down some things you notice about the narrative. You will probably notice the bits of bad storytelling. In games, you shouldn't even notice the good storytelling. It should just blend in with the overall experience.

For instance, watch out for particularly long-winded tomes or that noticeably mechanical NPC dialogue where the character spells out the quest without an ounce of juicy character to wash that jagged pill down.

It's on a sunny Sunday morning that I'm editing and expanding this chapter. Last night I played Deep Sky: Derelicts. It was 75 percent off on Steam and I'd heard that it's basically Darkest Dungeon in space. Alas, if only that were true. Mechanically, it's a decent squad tactics rogue-like game. The artwork is great too. An eye-catching combo of comic and macabre. But the storytelling... ugh. The first thing I noticed is that every human character sounds the same. There's no voice-over to help differentiate character, so it just comes down to the dialogue text. The robot and AI tones are notably different from the human tones. I'll give the narrative designer credit there. But the robot and AI dialogues all sound like each other also. Even though there are many characters in the game, there are only two voice styles that I've encountered so far.

So that's something to watch out for. Are the characters well differentiated or do they all sound like one person, namely... the writer.

> LOSE THE PLOT

I wouldn't worry too much about the plot in the games you are playing. This may be contrary to a lot of things you've heard about writing for games, but plot shouldn't be your chief concern in producing a satisfying narrative for a player.

Plot is the governing principle of cinema, novels, television and theatre, but it is most definitely not the most important part of the game story. We need to be on the lookout for all the telltale signs of an effective story experience.

Immersion is your primary aim as a narrative designer.

You need to help the player forget about the real world, help them switch off the analytical side of the brain, and just immerse themselves in the game world. And to do that, every bit of that game world has to make sense. Now, I don't mean that it has to make sense immediately to the player. I just mean that every part of the game world has to make story sense to every other part of the game world.

So if the player character is encouraged to rummage through rubbish bins to find ammunition for his rocket launcher, then we have a serious issue with the integrity of that world's story experience. Yes, I'm looking at you, Bioshock Infinite. If the bystanders in your FPS game all shout the same thing when the gunfire starts up, no matter what culture, age or general disposition they are, then that's hindering, not helping, the narrative. Yes, I'm looking at you Deus Ex: Human Revolution.

It's the same if you're playing something like Civilization. Every unit, every tech advancement, every piece of NPC advisor wisdom needs to feel like it's all part of the same world.

World integrity is definitely the responsibility of the narrative designer. As you play, ask yourself how the game world feels. Does it feel complete? Are there moments where a sharp piece of the world jabs you, reminding you that you're 'just playing a game'?

> WRITE

You've probably heard the 10,000 hours principle already, along with a whole raft of mastery theories that get bandied about these days. "Writing has a 10 year apprenticeship" is one that you'll probably hear a lot too. And mostly these principles apply to game writing, just like any other form of writing. So the emphasis here is on writing and how much you end up doing of this particularly nefarious task.

If you've got a limited amount of time, like most of us, then it's probably not wise to spend it on lectures, tutorials, and writing essays about narrative design. The more fiction you write, the better.

Let's go deeper into the writing in the next chapter.

WRITING THEM WORDIES_

> SHORT AND SWEET

Short form writing is the way to get your brain thinking like a narrative designer's brain.

While novels are wonderful things and great sources of inspiration and information, they have all the time in the world to express themselves. In narrative design, your job is to say what you have to say succinctly so you can get out of the way of the player and let them do their thing.

As mentioned before, the best result is when your player doesn't even know they're being told a story. Brush up on your poetry, flash fiction, drama skits, snappy jokes and short stories. Short form writing encourages you to practice getting to the point, making it well, and then getting out as fast as humanly possible.

I've seen instances where novelists, particularly fantasy and science fiction novelists, have tried to jump straight into narrative design. My experience has been that they create excellent documents at the lore level development on a grand, high concept level, but fall flat when it comes to creating an interactive story and the actual pieces of narrative that need to go into the game to express that high concept lore in hands-on terms. In fact, I've been hired quite a few times to come in and tidy up after said novelists. No offense intended to them. They've been excellent writers. It's just been a square peg to a round hole situation.

If you are primarily a novelist at this stage, then I would highly recommend practicing short form fiction before diving into a narrative design project. If you're primarily a short form writer, then you're well positioned already.

> BE A MIMIC

And what about developing your individual, authentic voice as a writer? Well, narrative design is primarily a collaborative business. Yes, sometimes you'll receive the creative control necessary to forge a unique voice for a specific game, but those opportunities are few.

Versatility is the key in writing for games. I guess that's where I can thank Shortland Street for teaching me a few important things, skills that have stood me in good stead when it comes to writing for games.

The first is that I learned to wrangle a large cast of characters who varied dramatically in the way they spoke, behaved, and in the stories that you could tell about them. There were the romantic leads, the handsome and beautiful surgeons of wealth, power and daring medical deeds. There were non-binary nurses exploring the issues of sexuality and cultural identity. There were ethnic minorities navigating their way through post-colonial New Zealand society. And there were villains of all sorts, ranging from comedic gossips and ruthless social climbers through to mad scientists and serial killers.

Overarching all this character variety, a serial drama has a certain 'voice' that needs to be expressed and maintained. In

Shortland Street's specific case, it's more of a 'one size fits all' approach. The show tries to appeal to as many demographics as possible. And it can do that by having multiple storylines and multiple characters. A viewer may not identify with the surgeon romance plotline and might well enjoy the teens-in-trouble storyline.

If you're working with games that are going for mass appeal then it's the 'one size fits all' voice you will deal with. Sprawling AAA titles like Assassin's Creed: Odyssey do this. There are so many NPCs and quests that you're bound to find something in there you can identify with and enjoy.

With Indie projects, you'll probably find that the creator has strong and specific views about the concepts of the story and how they want them expressed. Again, speaking from experience, I've seen the tragic results of a writer who comes in and tries to override that creative vision with their own. The result is often a fall-out, lots of bad feeling, a legal tangle, and, at the end of the day, the poor old game still needs a story.

Like any other commercial writer, the narrative designer is there to serve the client. It pays to ask a lot of questions up front so you can establish what sort of voice the client wants for their game. Then it's up to you to try and express that voice. The beauty of this process is that you get to practice a lot of different storytelling styles and become a highly versatile writer.

Suffice to say that the writer of any game needs to adapt themselves to the style of that game, not the other way around.

What I'd recommend is this. It's a fairly common writing exercise that I've seen offered in many writing books. Find some different short fiction. Try to get examples from as many styles as possible and then have a go at creating your own versions of them. Change the subject but have a go at writing this fresh topic in the style of one of those short form pieces.

For instance, take the style of a poem like The Highwayman

by 'unknown author' and write about a hunted werewolf instead
of a hunted highwayman. Or grab a Neil Gaiman or Stephen
King short story, change the setting, and switch out the gender
and culture of the main character for something new. Then have
a go at recreating that short story with the new elements in
place.

Is this plagiarism? No, because you're not going to publish it
and pretend that it is your own work. This is just practice at wran-
gling multiple voices.

Every game you write for will have a different voice, and that
voice will be decided upon by the creator of that game. Or in the
case of mid-size and AAA games, a committee of creators that will
often include a publisher.

Your job, as a narrative designer, is to take the game devs' ideas
and turn them into a game story.

> INTERACTIVE FICTION

There is one form of storytelling that I think every narrative
designer should master, and that's interactive fiction.

Why?

Because it's the perfect combination of writing and interactivity, and because it's relatively easy to produce. Well, when I say
'easy', I mean that it's cheap to produce. Since you're just dealing
with text, you need not worry about all the bells and whistles that
would normally go into making a game.

If you've never heard of interactive fiction, then I strongly
suggest you play Guardian Māia. You can download the first part
for free from the Appstore and Google Play. Outfits like Inkle, Tin
Man, Choice of Games and Cubus also have excellent examples of
the genre. You could even search out some old classics like the
Infocom games.

As of writing this, interactive fiction (IF) has experienced a significant renaissance, which is lucky for you, so there's lots of material around to study and gain inspiration from.

But what if you're just starting out? Well, an interactive fiction piece makes a wonderful writing sample for a fledgling narrative designer. It not only shows the quality of your writing but also whether you can put the player in the driver's seat and design a cool story experience for them.

It'll help you develop your ability to wrangle an interactive story–something which doesn't come naturally. It's something you really have to practice, something you have to encourage your brain to do so it can form the correct neural pathways.

To be honest, in the early days of my career, I found it hard to keep multiple pathways in my head so I could navigate my way through the design of an interactive story. This may have been because I watched more TV and read more novels than I played games and gamebooks in my early years. I don't know. I *did* make a point of playing every interactive fiction I could get my hands on during the 80s and 90s, but alas, there just weren't that many around.

And because I had a master of film script writing and had worked in serial drama, I initially approached narrative design with a very linear mindset. This was fine while I was developing simple quest chains and overarched plot lines, but became a bit of a problem when I had to design a quest that had multiple ways of being completed. I have in mind the 'three bandits' quest from Path of Exile.

> BOGGLING BRANCHES

The quest was called 'Lords of Larceny'. The player had to collect three pieces of a magical pyramid artefact. To get those pieces they had to visit three bandit lords, or more accurately, two bandit lords and a bandit lady. Oak, Kraityn and Alira. Each bandit possessed one of the three pieces, which would have been simple enough if you had to kill them, as is most often the case in an action RPG.

However, in our dubious wisdom, we decided it would be cool if you could also ally with a bandit. Your new cutthroat friend would then ask you to kill the other bandits and collect their pyramid pieces. The bandit would then combine the pieces and give the player a magical buff as a reward.

And to make matters even more complicated, we also had an NPC in the local hub called Eramir who wanted you to take the simpler action RPG approach; kill all three bandit lords and deliver the three pieces to him. Eramir would then combine the pieces and give the player a different magical buff. It may seem simple enough, but it can end up being a mind-boggling number of outcomes.

[⬚]

To show how complicated this can get, here's the dialogue from Kraityn, one of the Lords of Larceny.

> LORDS OF LARCENY DIALOGUE_ KRAITYN

If the PC has no BANDIT ALLY and both Oak and Alira are still alive…
Kraityn: [Kraityn's Rivals]
You're trouble. I like that. Know what I don't like? Oak and Alira, and their thieving mongrels. They keep taking what's mine. I'm thinking you could do something about that.
What's in it for you? The amulets around Oak and Alira's necks. The ones like mine here. There's power in them beyond reckoning.
Take two heads, take two amulets, bring them to me, and take half the power.
That add up right for you?

If the PC has not ALLIED and has already killed Oak...

Kraityn:

Heard you toppled a big tree. Handy work, that. And if you can chop down an Oak, you can pull out a weed. The weed's got a name... Alira, and I'm sick of seeing her in my garden.

What's in it for you? The amulets around Oak and Alira's necks. The ones like mine here. There's power in them beyond reckoning.

I'm thinking you got one already from old lumber-for-brains. Make it two, bring them to me, and take half the power for yourself.

That add up right for you?

If the PC has not ALLIED and has already killed Alira...

Kraityn:

Heard you pulled a weed out of my garden... the Alira thistle. Handy work, that. Now there's a tree needs choppin' down too. An Oak. He's blocking my sun.

What's in it for you? The amulets around Oak and Alira's necks. The ones like mine here. There's power in them beyond reckoning.

I'm thinking you got one already from the slattern. Make it two, bring them to me, and take half the power for yourself.

That add up right for you?

If the PC has not ALLIED and has already killed Oak AND Alira...

Kraityn:

Heard you been doing some serious gardening around the place. Felled a big, dumb Oak and plucked an Alira thistle from her foul bed.

And I'm thinking you got a couple of amulets in your pockets. Ones like mine here. There's power in them, you know. But only when all three get to dance together.

I'm not greedy, mind. I'm willing to split that power with you, right down the middle. Hand me those amulets and let's see what fate has in store for us.

If the PC hands over the amulets...

[Kraityn combines the three pieces of the key and there's a resulting power up effect.]

Kraityn:

Ah, sweeter than mother's milk.

[Referring to the now complete key artefact.]

Might as well take this pretty husk with you. Something to remember me by. Nice working with you, matey. I'd wish you luck on your travels, but from what I seen, you won't be needing it.

If the PC fights Kraityn for all three amulets...

Kraityn:

Like I figured, first time I saw you. You're trouble. And trouble don't play nice with others.

Guess what. I'm a bit troubled, myself.

[The fight is on.]

If the PC has already ALLIED with Oak, and Alira is still alive...

Kraityn:

So you're Oak's lackey, are you? I could be wasting the last of my breath here, but you're barking up the wrong tree. Once he's done with you, your brains will be splattered over the nearest trunk.

Here's the truth of it. Oak and Alira, they care for nothing and no-one. Me? I care about a thing called Arithmetic. You go take two heads and two amulets, bring them to me, and you get half the power.

That add up right to you?

If the PC has already ALLIED with Oak, and Alira is dead...

Kraityn:

Heard you pulled a weed out of my garden... the Alira thistle. Handy work, that. But you're Oak's lackey, are you? I could be wasting the last of my breath here but... you're barking up the wrong tree. Once he's done with you, your brains will be splattered over the nearest trunk.

Here's the truth of it. Alira cares for nothing and no-one. Me? I care about a thing called Arithmetic. You go take one head, bring me two amulets, and I'll give you half the power.

That add up right to you?

If the PC has already ALLIED with Alira, and Oak is still alive...

Kraityn:

So you're Alira's lap dog, are you? I could be wasting the last of my breath here, but you're chasing the wrong tale. Once Alira's done with you those brave guts of yours'll be steaming on the ground.

Here's the truth of it. Oak and Alira, they care for nothing and no-one. Me? I care about a thing called Arithmetic. You go take two heads and two amulets, bring them to me, and you get half the power.

That add up right to you?

If the PC has already ALLIED with Alira, and Oak is dead...

Kraityn:

Heard you felled a big tree. Handy work, that. But you're Alira's lap dog, are you? I could be wasting the last of my breath here... you're chasing the wrong tale. Once Alira's done with you those brave guts of yours'll be steaming on the ground.

Here's the truth of it. Alira cares for nothing and no-one. Me? I care about a thing called Arithmetic. You go take one head, bring me two amulets, and I'll give you half the power.

That add up right to you?

If the PC decides to ALLY with Kraityn, and Oak and Alira still live...

Kraityn:

No pain, no gain, I once heard someone say. Make sure it's Oak and Alira's pain now, won't you? And lots of it.

If the PC decides to ALLY with Kraityn, and only Oak still lives...

Kraityn:

No pain, no gain, I once heard someone say. Make sure it's Oak's pain now, won't you? And lots of it.

If the PC decides to ALLY with Kraityn, and only Alira still lives...

Kraityn:

No pain, no gain, I once heard someone say. Make sure it's Alira's pain now, won't you? And lots of it.

If the PC has ALLIED with Kraityn and killed NEITHER Oak nor Alira...

Kraityn:

Don't think we've got anything more to talk about, do we? Bring me a head or two. That's always a good conversation starter.

If the PC has ALLIED with Kraityn and killed Oak but not Alira...

Kraityn:

Heard you felled a big tree and got yourself one of the amulets. Handy work, that.

But you don't seem the kind to leave a job half done. If you can chop down an Oak, you can pull out a weed.

The weed's got a name... Alira, and I'm sick of seeing her in my garden.

If the PC has ALLIED with Kraityn and killed Alira but not Oak...

Kraityn:

Heard you pulled a weed out of my garden and got yourself one of the amulets. Handy work, that.

But you don't seem the kind to leave a job half done. Remember there's a tree needs chopping down. Goes by the name of Oak. He's blocking my sun.

If the PC is ALLIED with Kraityn and has killed both Alira and Oak...

Kraityn:

My garden's all tidy, just like that. I knew you were just the kind of trouble I needed.

Now, hand me those amulets and let's see what fate has in store for us.

If the PC hands over the amulets...

[Kraityn combines the three pieces of the key and there's a resulting power up effect.]

Kraityn:

Ah, sweeter than mother's milk.

[Referring to the now complete key artefact.]

Might as well take this pretty husk with you. Something to remember me by.

Nice working with you, matey. I'd wish you luck on your travels but from what I seen, you won't be needing it.

If the PC is ALLIED with Kraityn but decides to fight Kraityn for all three amulets...

Kraityn:

And I thought we really had something going here. Should have known. Trouble and loyalty aren't common bedfellows. No matter. An easy mistake to fix.

[The fight is on.]

Remember, I wrote this back in 2011, before I had any interactive narrative tools other than Google Docs to work with. Nowadays I'd write this up in Ink Script where values could track each different state and make slight adjustments to the text accordingly. I would take a fraction of the time and we'd end up with a prototype of the above dialogues that we could actually play.

Back then, in 2011, it was a copy, paste and tweak exercise. Laborious, but I got there.

And the above example doesn't even come close to the responsive narrative complexity of something like Inkles 80 Days or the dialogue options in a game like Oxenfree. The current day tools help, but it's your brain that has to grow the neural pathways so you can hold multiple concurrent realities in your head.

And for that, practice *does* make perfect.

GETTING THE GIG_

How do you *actually* go about getting a narrative design gig?

Naturally, it's much easier once you have a few projects under your belt. You can feature these projects on a LinkedIn profile and you can present all of your work on a website. That's what's worked for me so far. I've tried other platforms, some specifically focused on the general media industry, some on the games industry itself, and nothing has outperformed my LinkedIn profile and website. In fact, nothing is what I've received from every other platform I've tried.

Except for Facebook. I've received a wee bit of work via Facebook, and mostly because I've friended other game devs there. But we're honestly talking tiny.

You should definitely fire up a LinkedIn profile and a website even if your project list consists of student projects and freebie work for start-ups. Proof of work is proof of work, whether or not you got paid for it.

However, there quickly comes a time when you have to charge for your work. The reality of the industry is that you will need to do some free work first just to prove yourself. But that does not mean work for free for other people for the mystical payment of "exposure". In fact, this kind of promise seems increasingly fragrant with the pungent odors of bovine faeces.

Everybody wants your blood, sweat and tears for free. So rather than committing all that effort to other people's projects, I would highly recommend putting that energy into your own projects.

This advice is born of hard-earned experience on my part. I've spent a lot of time and energy on Kickstarter campaigns and Indie projects that went absolutely nowhere. Rarely has a pro bono gig turned into a paying gig.

There are exceptions, so I'm not saying that you should never give away your work for free. Just be very careful before you do. Do your due diligence, only work with teams who have prior professional experience (where possible), and put a firm limit on the time you will put into a pro bono job.

Even if you have a long list of projects behind you, you will sometimes need to write an audition piece or provide a tangible sample of your work.

> INK SCRIPT

For the latter, I would again suggest creating interactive fiction pieces that show off both your writing skills and your ability to wrangle branching and basic mechanics.

My favorite tool for this is Ink Script, an open source scripting language. You can create your interactive stories in their free Inky editor, export them as html files, and play them on a website. Or, if you know an expert in Unity, Ink has a Unity interface, making it doable to create a professional quality IF game that you can export to multiple platforms, including mobile.

Despite its obvious technical advantages, Ink has a strong community around it, and it's the only IF I've used that allows you to still feel like you're writing. With others, it's all nodes and diagrams. With Ink Script, it's a beautiful blank page, begging for words.

Okay, enough romanticizing from me. See for yourself. I've created six free Ink Script tutorials to get you started.

www.edmcrae.com/article/learning-ink-script-tutorial-one

> AUDITION PIECES

For the former, the audition piece, I've provided a sample (below) for you to absorb and attempt.

Audition pieces have two natural stages to them.

> ONE. UNDERSTANDING THE BRIEF

Your audition prompts should let you know what narrative style the client wants.

That's why it's so important to read the brief carefully, and preferably several times. Before you even write that first word, you need to be confident of the voice that you're attempting to portray.

If the potential client / employer is giving you a week or so to complete the test, which they should, then try to spend some time playing their previous games. But that's only if those games are like what they are asking in the audition. If they are trying something new for their studio, ask them to recommend some games similar to what they are hoping to do. By playing these games, if only for the first hour of each game, you'll get a good idea of the story experience they are hoping for.

In fact, YouTube Let's Plays are a real time saver on that front. Since audition pieces are usually free, you want to get the maximum amount of understanding from the minimum time investment. Let's Plays enable you to fast forward the repetitive bits and get a good overview of the story experience while avoiding all that puzzling, grinding and/or dying.

> TWO. STICK TO THE BRIEF

This is not the time to show the client the error of their ways or try to open their eyes to new and innovative forms of storytelling. You can do that once you have the gig.

What the client wants to know is whether you can write what they want you to write. From your portfolio they can already see that you can write what you want to write. They may also see that you can write what other people wanted you to write. But that's still a far cry from knowing that you can deliver the story experience that they are specifically aiming for.

An audition isn't about showing that you are a good writer.

It's about proving that you are the right writer for the job.

> THREE. HUH?

I know I only said there were two stages. This third stage is far more about you than it is about the gig. It's the self-reflection stage that comes after the audition.

Once you've finished writing your audition piece, you need to ask yourself a few questions.

Was it fun to write?

Could you write in this style for many hundreds of hours?

If you hated the writing experience for this audition, then this probably isn't the narrative design gig for you.

Think of a good audition piece as being an audition for both sides. You're sussing out whether you want to work for them just as much as they are sussing out whether they want to work with you.

> WELCOME TO THE DEMON DAYS WRITER'S TEST!

Imagine I am the producer at a mid-level game development company who specialises in dark AARPGs.

Me: Write what we want you to write or we will drop you like a Twi'lek dancer into the Rancor pit.

Is that the rattling of chains and clanking of manacles I hear? Yes! The trial has begun!

However... before you delve into this audition piece, a word of warning to you.

Be careful of how many hours you sink into it, or any other audition piece. As a rule of thumb, I usually set a limit of around two to three hours for an audition. If it's a big game that I really want to write for, and that could foreseeably provide me with a lot of work, I might push the investment up to around four to five hours. But no more. If you are a freelance narrative designer, you have a business to run and can't afford to be throwing your valuable time around with wanton abandon.

And no, there's no pressure for you to do the audition that follows because there will be no one to appraise it. It's simply good practice. But like all forms of writing, practice makes 'perfect'. Actually, that's a silly phrase because there's no such thing as perfection. Practice makes a professional.

Good luck!

> DEMON DAYS STYLE GUIDELINES

Guideline 1

Make it dark!

Make it eloquent.

Would Christopher Lee have been able to deliver your lines with gravitas and ominous portent?

 As the light of our age dwindles and dies, the darkness rises to usurp its once blinding tyranny."

Guideline 2

Make it epic!

 Grasp this fate with all your strength until its lifeblood erupts through your fingers."

Guideline 3

Make it romantic, in a melancholy way.

 The steel gleams wet with tears wept freely in these fields of strife and sorrow."

Guideline 4

Make it funny!

Sometimes a little humor is needed to relieve the tension, even in dark fantasy.

 I would take the roar of a dragon over the tax collector's incessant bleat."

Guideline 5

Make it short!

Our players haven't come to our game to read tomes and listen to speeches. They're here to kill demons. The story elements must be brief so that they won't slow the overall pace of the game.

> PROCEDURAL GENERATION

Much of Demon Days will be procedurally generated. The game world will never be the same for any two playthroughs. Therefore, we don't have the scope to create large set piece events. Story events will need to be self contained and mobile, able to remain effective when placed almost anywhere on a particular level.

Bad Example:

 Beware this northern path for that way leads straight down the arch demon's throat."

Good Example:

 Your path is paved in doom, for it leads straight down the arch demon's throat."

To the task at hand!

So here's the Demon Days setting for you. It's a post-apocalyptic land stained with tragedy and crawling with evil.

A once mighty nation stood, only ruins and haunting memories remain. Centuries ago, the demons rose and tore this fair land down. Yet ancient riches and powerful secrets remain for any brave enough to seek them. For any willing to face the demons and take back that which was lost.

> NPC DIALOGUE

Step 1: Write a profile for an NPC about to explore a ruined temple. We find the NPC at the entranceway to a ruined temple where captured humans were sacrificed by lesser demons for the purpose of summoning greater demons. The temple is still full of tortured phantoms and roaming monstrosities.

Please note: Although the temple dungeon will be procedurally generated, the temple entranceway will be in a fixed location. This NPC will always be found at the temple.

In your NPC profile, please include...

- Specify gender, culture and age.
- A basic physical description.
- As a handy shortcut, find an 'Inspiration Reference'. This is a historical figure or a well-known character from a film or television series.
- Describe any special characteristics and motives that this NPC might have.
- Why have they come to this forsaken land?
- What do they want from this temple?
- Are they an honest character or are they hiding a dark secret?

Here are a few options that you might want to use as starters. We're happy for you to come up with your own too.

- A wizard seeking a magical artefact.
- A ghost who needs to solve its past so it can rest in peace.
- A dying adventurer who wants to see their quest completed.
- A wandering bard looking for inspiration for a new song.

Step 2: Write an Introductory dialogue for your NPC. This

dialogue should be from 100 to 150 words and must include the NPC's:

- Name.
- Greeting for the player.
- Reason (real or supposed) for being at that location.

Please Note: While we refer to the 'dialogue' of our NPCs, we actually mean 'monologue'. The player's character is a silent protagonist and therefore cannot be heard responding to the NPC.

Step 3: Write the 'Quest Offer' dialogue for your NPC. This dialogue should be from 100 to 150 words and must include:

- A Quest Item that the NPC wishes the player to get from the ruined temple.
- An explanation (or cover story) for why the NPC needs the Quest Item.
- A brief description of the Boss Demon the player will need to slay to get the Quest Item.
- The reward the player will receive upon successful completion of the quest.

Step 4: Write the 'Quest Reward' dialogue for your NPC. This dialogue will play once the player has delivered the Quest Item to the NPC. It should be from 50 to 100 words and must include...

- Acceptance of the Quest Item.
- Congratulations on completion of the quest and acknowledgement of the Boss Demon's defeat.
- Delivery of the promised reward.

> FLAVOR TEXT

Because of the size constraints on our text boxes for items, we'll need a maximum of 20 words per flavor text.

Step 1: Axes of Executioner's Block. In the Executioner's Block level, the demon mobs have a percentage chance to drop a set of Arcane Axes once wielded by the executioners' guild. Each axe's flavor text should refer to crime and punishment, and the mercy of a quick, clean death.

Hatchet:
Throwing Axe:
Hewing Axe:
Battle Axe:
Executioner's Axe:

Step 2: Historical Figure Flavor. Continuing with our executioner's guild, let's create a full set of armour for a Death Lord, a powerful executioner and a member of the dreaded Council of the Axe.

- Name this historical figure and write a brief history (up to 100 words) or their rise to power within the executioner's guild.
- Provide an epic execution-related name for each armor base type and then write a piece of flavor text for each item.

Here, let's make it a quote, so the format will be:
"Epic quote." - Title Name of Place

Example:

Heads will roll." - Lord Carver of Grimsby

Executioner's Hood:
Chestplate:
Gauntlets:
Cuisses:
Boots:
Ring:
Amulet:

> STORY GLYPH

A fragment of story that the player accesses during play. Notes and books, graffiti and hieroglyphics, road signs and 'All Dead Here' warnings. All these are story glyphs of one form or another.

We'd like you to write a tome of 80 to 100 words. It's a memoir written by the same Death Lord whose armor you have just finished adding flavor text to.

This Death Lord is lamenting the corruption that now pollutes his beloved guild. While once the Council of the Axe upheld justice absolute, it now does the bidding of a tyrant king.

The Blunted Axe
Position:Executioners Guild Hall
Description: An ominous book bound in black leather. It can be found at the foot of the Death Lord's once imposing statue. The statue has been split in two by some unholy force.
Text: [Insert tome text here.]

You're done!

I suggest featuring this audition piece in your online portfolio. It's a great way for prospective clients / employers to see a sample of your writing. If you don't have an online profile or website yet, create one. This is essential if you want to make it as a freelancer. More about that coming up!

And if you don't want to target the dark ARPG market, you can always set yourself a brief using the same basic structure. Create a game concept, something you would love to write for, and build the audition piece around that.

Tailor your audition piece to show off your narrative design strengths and to communicate the game gigs you hope to write for.

Good luck!

THE NARRATIVE DESIGN BUSINESS_

We've all been warned not to keep all of our eggs in one basket. But if you're a staff writer for a video game company, that's *exactly* what you are doing. I've never been a staff writer so I've never experienced the stress and upset of a sudden layoff. Yet I've witnessed that turmoil among fellow writers. I won't go into names and companies, to protect those involved, but suffice to say... it wasn't pretty.

Go freelance!

That's been my solution to sustaining a 10 year career as a narrative designer. I've never had a single client. Even in the early days, when I was doing the majority of my writing work for Path of Exile, I still took on other projects. As a result, I gradually built up an experience portfolio that covers everything from quest design for a hardcore viking ARPG (Rune 2) through to the fantastical contextualization of psychometric testing (Owiwi).

The immense diversity of games means that, as a freelancer, you are *never* putting all of your eggs in one basket. The games industry *as a whole* as grown rapidly over the last ten years, but within the industry, games genres have their own boom and bust cycles. Point-and-click adventures games might see a surge of popularity one year and get absolutely no attention the following year. Mid-core ARPGs might do really well for a while but might then have all their players stolen by a AAA ARPG release. As of writing this, games about pandemics are topping the charts thanks to fears about Covid-19, but will that popularity last beyond the current crisis? Probably not.

As a freelancer, you are well positioned to sail through these choppy waters. If work in one genre dries up you can quickly switch your focus to another genre. The more variation in the projects you complete, the more versatility you show, the more chance there is that potential clients will see something similar to their project in your portfolio and ask you to help them.

How do you make game devs aware of your existence in the first place? How do you make yourself discoverable? My strategy is a simple one, but it's worked so far.

Website + LinkedIn profile

My website, www.edmcrae.com, is where I explain what I can offer and what I've achieved so far. It's also where I blog about narrative design. Yes, many will say "the blog is dead, long live video/audio" but my blog has been how I've established showcased my hard-earned knowledge. Like anyone, game devs will go searching on the internet. If you're providing the answers for those questions via a blog, then they you have a good chance of being found.

I won't go into the specifics of blog marketing here. Theres a *ton* of information out there already, written by marketers far more savvy than me. I'll just give you an example of something that *has* worked for me.

This article has netted me more traffic than anything else I've written on my website.

https://www.edmcrae.com/article/what-is-a-narrative-designer

It's the 15th of March, 2020, and I've just put "narrative designer" into a Google Incognito search. The above article has the number two spot in the search results, pipped at the post by Wikipedia.

Pillar Posts, I've heard them called. Blog posts that target a specific searcher question and get decent traffic as a result. So try to think about what game story solutions game devs might be searching the internet for. Talk to devs and ask them what questions regularly come up for them. Once you have a few idea, write the posts *on your own website* and see what happens. The results won't be immediate, but if you've picked the right answers, the traffic should come. Get enough traffic and the gig inquiries may follow.

I emphasize *your own website* because you want to be answering to the search engines and *only* the search engines. For instance, after all of the discoverability changes Facebook has made of late in favor of increasing their ad revenues, I would not recommend FB for promoting your services. Yes, it should be part of your overall strategy, but I certainly wouldn't be putting all of my eggs in *that* basket. Not unless you're prepared to spend a pretty penny on boosted posts and advertising.

LinkedIn has been my second best source of work, and I repost all of my blog posts there for the same reasons.

Discoverability.

Proof of expertise.

Sound like hard work? It is! It means creating a whole bunch of content for free. But I love talking about narrative design almost as much as I love doing it. Here's hoping you feel the same way.

The last thing to consider, when going freelance, is your infrastructure. There are a few boxes you need to tick to make yourself remote-ready and financially solid.

1. High spec PC or laptop - You need to be able to play game builds.
2. Excellent internet - Sharing files needs to be quick and easy, and you need to be able to easily download game builds.
3. Cloud Services - Once again, file sharing is vital. I mostly use Google Drive and Dropbox, but be prepared to use anything that your clients might favor.
4. Communication Options - Skype, Discord, Google Hangouts... whatever your clients prefer. Much of your communication will be through email and chat, but there's nothing like a face to face to work out the more complex narrative design issues.
5. Limited Liability Company - Pay tax *after* expenses.
6. Accountant - There to make sure you *do* pay your taxes.
7. Time Tracker - Narrative Design is a 'billable hours' business, just like a lawyer or accountant. This business might be all 'fun and games' but you're doing a job and need to get paid for your time.

So the mental agility you develop through narrative design will also help you find more and more narrative design work.

Yes, I'm totally biased because I've been a freelancer for my entire career so far. But here's one last reason, just for the record.

Of the legion of game dev companies out there is this $120 billion dollar industry, the vast majority are Indie or mid-level outfits who don't need a staff writer for their project. This is usually to do with scale. A 100 hour sandbox RPG may well need a team writers working full time. A Match 3 mobile game about monster collection does not. Neither does a 10 hour, story-driven puzzler. Most narrative needs are *at-the-time* needs. Sometimes it'll be at the beginning to help with the game's story context. Sometimes it'll be at the end to write in-game dialogue. Sometimes it'll be in the middle to include narrative in the procedural generation system. But rarely does a small to mid-level game need a writer *all the time*.

That's where freelancers are a dev's 'Godsend'. You can work on their narrative needs while also working on twelve other games over the course of a year. You're there when they need you, but you're not there, twiddling your thumbs and costing them money, when you're *not* needed.

And it's a win for you too. Why? Because it's far more likely that twelve game devs will need a bit of story than one game dev will need a lot of story. Sure, you won't end up with your name on a fancy AAA game like an Assassin's Creed or Dragon Age, but does it really matter? Wouldn't you rather just get paid to do something you really enjoy?

Although, you also have to rethink your definition of enjoyment, rewrite your sense of creative 'fun'.

Picture this, if you will. Sitting down at your keyboard or microphone, losing yourself in writing for a solid three-hour block. The words flow from your mind, tongue and fingertips. Characters, worlds and plot form like an oil painting in your head. Or perhaps you feel like a sculptor, chipping away, a beautiful statue revealing itself out of the raw rock, smiling at you, beatific and grateful for bringing it into the world.

You're in a state of 'flow', just you and the story, a true and blissful conduit of the universal consciousness, Greek muses, creative soul, or whatever else you believe in.

Narrative Design is more like plumbing than 'flow'.

Yes, occasionally, I'll have that immersive writing experience, when writing up a lore document or a longer dialogue for a cut scene, but those moments are few. The romantic notion of the lone writer happily immersed in imaginary worlds, sustained by lovely royalty payments, doesn't really stack up as a narrative designer. Maybe it will, but at the time of writing this, it's not really a 'thing'.

> CREATIVE CONSTRUCTION

Writing for games is more an experience in 'creative construction' than it is in 'artistic expression'. If you're an 'artiste' whose every word is precious and a beautiful gift of creation, then you will probably find the games industry somewhere between frustrating and utterly maddening. But if you enjoy knocking out stories, have a ton of ideas you don't mind sharing, and are cool with people telling you what to write and when to write it, often in very specific terms, then maybe this is the career for you.

If you've had experience as a copywriter or been part of a writing team for a TV series, then I'm preaching to the converted. You know what it's like to create work that you don't own and to follow briefs that you often have no say in. If not, then brace yourself, because that's the world of narrative design, nine times out of ten.

That said, in the Indie world, my experience has been one of creative satisfaction. I've had a lot more creative control when working with Indie developers, and that's why I've written mostly for Indies throughout my entire career. But they're still not 'my' stories. And they still have to be constructed narb by narb, brick by brick. Very few moments of writing flow. Lots of problem-solving and tinkering.

But as we know, construction has its own flow state. Any Lego fiend (like me) will attest to that! It can definitely be fun. It's just a different type of fun to what a linear, non-interactive writer might be used to.

I'm not trying to put you off. I just want you to go into this business with your eyes open.

Freelance to multiple clients.
Work within the briefs.
Find creative satisfaction with the constraints.
Get paid well for your efforts.
Narrative design is a business. Treat it like a business.

UNDERSTANDING GAMERS_

> DO GAMERS EVEN LIKE STORY?

> WHY DO WE LOVE RPGS?

GAMER ARCHETYPES_

You've probably already heard of the three *general* categories of player.

1. Casual
2. Hardcore
3. Midcore

Here are my somewhat paraphrased definitions, but remember these are *not* hard-and-fast definitions of player behavior. Players will show one type as a general preference, a way they naturally engage with a game, but they may still dabble in the other types on any given day, depending on their mood and the attractiveness of various elements within these other game types.

> CASUAL

Your casual gamer is looking for fun and distraction in the moment. They'll never stay in the game long enough to engage with a plotline, although many will enjoy an interesting story context. They favor quickly solved puzzles and repeatable actions with instant rewards attached. Time investment is measured in minutes for casual play.

- e.g. Mana Monsters, Splash!, Flip This House.

There's plenty of story work to be had with casual games, especially for game writers. But story will always take fourth place after the 'three Ms'.

1. Mechanics
2. Multiplayer
3. Monetization

> HARDCORE

These gamers are *seriously* into complex and highly challenging game mechanics. They put in a BIG time investment! Hundreds of hours.

- e.g. Path of Exile, Rune 2, Bloodbourne.

Hardcores are *almost only* interested in gameplay. They'll often click through dialogue, no matter how well it's written and voiced. And don't even think about asking them to read something that's not a skill description or an item stat summary.

Hardcores are generally NOT the target audience for narrative. They don't take kindly to cut scenes or any other form of storytelling that interrupts their gameplay. It's best to just make sure they get the information they need to keep playing and then get the heck out of their way.

> LORE JUNKIES (A SUBGROUP OF HARDCORE)

There's an interesting exception to your classic hardcore, and that's the Lore Junky.

Lore Junkies will listen to everything and read *everything*. They take a 'hardcore' approach to story, getting a kick out of discovering and understanding fictional histories and character backstories. They want full immersion in this fictional world, so getting them involved in narrative is like shooting fish in a barrel.

However, the payoff in user numbers is often small because they're relatively rare. That said, they're often extremely vocal about their love of a good game story, being the ones that launch into lengthy discussions about game lore in Reddit and other forums. This can do wonders for a game on the marketing front, so devs are often keen to keep these players happy by feeding them plenty of juicy lore to chew over.

> MIDCORE

Midcore players are *most definitely* a narrative designer's target audience.

They seek a challenge but don't have the time to sink into hardcore endeavors. They have tens of hours to invest rather than hundreds. They're the player type that's most interested in a balance of mechanics and story and are more likely to 'finish' a game's central plotline.

- e.g. Ashen, Witcher 3, Mad Max: Fury Road.

Midcores appreciate a balanced blend of gameplay and narrative. They love a good game mechanic, but rather than revelling in the buffs like hardcores, midcores need some context with their number crunching.

These players need to know why they're doing what they do in-game. They feel more comfortable when there's a purpose to their efforts, whether it is to save the land from ancient evils or wreak vengeance upon the arch-villain for slaughtering their family/village/household pet.

Midcores will engage with a voice-over if it's well written, professionally performed, and isn't too long winded. They read in-game text when it feels important to do so.

In fact, aside from Lore Junkies, midcores are the games industry's most avid engagers of in-game story content, and this is because their intentions often align with the scale of storytelling in games. Mechanics are simply more scalable than story, meaning that a thousand hours of gameplay is *much* cheaper and easier to produce than a thousand hours of narrative content.

Because midcores measure their gaming hours in the tens, story is the perfect return on their time investment. Story enables a sense of completion that procedural generation and endgame scenarios do not. Because their time is limited, midcores want their games to be limited too. And there's nothing quite so satisfying to a human brain as a completed story.

And although casual gamers make up most of the gaming industry's audience, especially in mobile, midcores are the next largest group.

But they are also the hardest to please because their preferences are more generalized. Hardcores won't even notice a shoddy story, such is their singular focus on the mechanics. Lore Junkies will forgive clunky mechanics if the world is fascinating enough. Midcores require harmony between story and mechanics.

They're looking for the 'Goldilocks' experience. Not too crunchy and not too soft, a 'just right' gaming experience. So it's up to us to understand their motivations and therefore cater to them.

That's why understanding your audience is so key to being a

successful narrative designer. You need to be as interested in psychology as you are in similes and sentence structure.

Unfortunately, gamer psychology is still an excruciatingly young field, so there isn't a lot of material out there to absorb, apart from the odd good book like Getting Gamers by Jamie Madigan.

That situation's getting better every day, but for now we narrative designers have to make our own observations and concoct our own psychological theories.

In the next chapter I'll explain one of my gamer motivation theories based on my years of gaming and game development, and my fascination with gamer culture.

Having a psych degree and a lifelong interest in human behavior has also helped me *a lot* when it comes to understanding gamers. But I'll be the first to admit that there's still *so* much to learn!

THE DIVINE ATTRACTION OF RPGS_

Let's do a little psychosocial case study, focusing on RPGs specifically. The reason being that understanding gamers is a massive part of the narrative designer's mindset.

To create effective game narratives, we need to get into the heads of gamers. We need to understand these strange beasties as best we can so we can satisfy their wants and positively inform their behaviors.

> WHY DO WE LOVE RPGS?

I'll put this to you. What if it's about the gods? Yes, Aphrodite and Zeus, Thor and Odin. I'm speaking from a strictly western perspective and those are the two pantheons that arise in games time and again. Greek and Norse. These are the examples I'll draw on, but there are many other divine influences besides them. They're just the ones that pop up in video games and Marvel movies.

Why do we love RPGs? Is it because we want to be 'godlike'?

> ATTENTION

During the Viking era, the population of the whole Scandinavian world was a few million, at most.

By 400BC, the population of the entire Greek world had reached around 13 million.

Joseph Smith and his Book of Mormon is revered by 14.8 million Mormons.

In 25BC, Emperor Augustus ruled a Roman Empire of 56.8 million citizens.

Pewdiepie has almost 89 million subscribers and his videos get between 6 million and 18 million views per day.

Pewdiepie gets more daily attention than the Greek and Norse gods combined during their religious heydays. Does Cthulhu get 6 to 18 million prayers per day? That's probably why the sea levels are rising. ;-)

Even the trailer for Thor: Ragnarok got 136 million views in only 24 hours. That's Chris Hemsworth pretending to be Thor. And not even the original Norse Thor. The Marvel version of Thor. Which makes me wonder if Disney/Marvel have ever paid the Scandinavian people for the right to make comics and movies out of the god they created? No, let's not open up that can of serpents.

If we convert the ancient concept of 'worship' into the modern concept of 'attention', then Pewdiepie and Chris Hemsworth receive up to ten times the amount of daily worship than Apollo or Thor ever did. I picked Apollo as the comparison to Pewdiepie because Apollo was variously recognized as a god of music, truth, prophecy, sun and light, and poetry. Yes, Apollo was an entertainer. But in actual fact, if we were to stick with Pewdiepie's cultural roots, then he's probably a cross between Odin (God of Knowledge) and Loki (Trickster God and Shapeshifter), with a bit more emphasis on Loki.

Following this logic, if receiving massive amounts of attention (worship) makes an individual godlike, then why do we give people like Pewdiepie and Chris Hemsworth so much attention?

I know this isn't yet relating directly to RPGs, but I'll get there soon, I promise.

> PIECE OF THE ACTION

We worship Pewdiepie and Thor because we want a piece of that action. By giving attention to Pewdiepie, by subscribing to his channel, we get to swim for a while in the invigorating ocean of attention that he inhabits. It's not just for entertainment. A cat playing a Playstation can be just as enjoyable as a Pewdiepie video. But even if that cat gets 1 million views, that's not the same as being part of an 89 million-strong ongoing viewership.

We watch a cat playing a Playstation, we laugh a bit and then we pretty much forget all about it. We watch a Pewdiepie video, we laugh and we forget everything except Pewdiepie himself. Try to remember what color the cat was three days later? Tough challenge. Try to visualize Pewdiepie? Piece of pie.

What about Chris Hemsworth as Thor? We give our attention to Thor because of the awesome things that Thor does. He performs massive feats of physical prowess. He shrugs off punishment that no mortal frame could bear. He calls down lightning from the sky. That's all serious godlike behavior. And through it all, you have Chris Hemsworth looking ridiculously composed and handsome. In Thor: Ragnarok, Hemsworth and Thor are one and the same. Before Hemsworth's Thor, you probably imagined a big, blond, bearded guy with a hammer, right? Nothing more specific than that. Now, when someone says "Thor", guess who you're more likely to visualize first. That's right. Chris Hemsworth.

I'm not saying we think Hemsworth is a god. I'm saying that we think of him as godlike. And by watching Thor: Ragnarok we get to spend some time in Thor's world and bask in Chris Hemsworth's godlike aura.

We get to forget our own frailties and lose ourselves in the worship of something godlike. Because to worship something godlike is to feel closer to something godlike.

What could be better than that?

> ROLE-PLAYING GOD

That's right. Being Thor.

Funnily enough, I haven't come across a decent game where you actually get to play as Thor. For this kind of experience, we have to turn back to the Greeks.

In God of War, you get to be Kratos.

KRATOS (Cratus) was the god or personified spirit (daemon) of strength, might, power and sovereign rule. He and his three siblings, Nike (Victory), Bia (Force) and Zelos (Rivalry), were winged enforcers for Zeus.

The latest God of War earned $131,000,000 in its launch month alone. If the entire Greek World of 400 BC gave Kratos the equivalent of a dollar a day in offerings, it would take over three months to accumulate what this one game earned in one.

Let's stick with Greek mythology but shift to a different game. Ubisoft hasn't disclosed its actual sales figures, but Assassin's Creed: Odyssey sold about 1.4 million copies in its first week after launch. It's easy to see how God of War is a godlike simulation. But what about Odyssey?

In Assassin's Creed: Odyssey you play a misthios–a person with a particular set of skills that can be hired for work. Basically, a freelancer. In this case, as Kassandra, your skills are that of a mercenary. Sounds all very humble until you experience her skills firsthand. It's not long before you are performing martial feats that Perseus and Heracles would have been proud of. Perseus and

Heracles are both sons of Zeus, and as demigods are the very definition of godlike.

And so is Kassandra. She is so far above being a frail human
that the comparison becomes almost meaningless. She's a
demigod.

> EARNING GODLINESS

But if Ubisoft had just handed all that power to the player at the
very beginning and said, "go be godlike", we would've had about
five minutes of fun and moved on to find something more
rewarding.

> RPGS. THE SECRET SAUCE

The secret sauce of a good RPG is that the player needs to earn
their godliness. Pewdiepie started with zero subscribers. Kassandra
can be knocked over by a humble wolf or bandit at the beginning
of Odyssey.

Godhood is actually pretty boring. Thor: Ragnarok is a two-
hour blast of fun, but could you watch that movie if it was 50
hours long? Could you watch Chris Hemsworth be awesome for
the equivalent of a busy working week?

I'm hoping your answer is "no".

The most engaging element of RPGs is that there is a clear,
measurable path to godliness. If we put in the time, practice the
gameplay, and learn about the game world through the story, then
we will eventually unlock those godlike abilities. As we pick up
better loot, we will even look godlike as we strut around in our
Legendary gear.

> PEWDIEPIE. LEVEL 1 YOUTUBER

These are Pewdiepie's humble beginnings, from Wikipedia - "In 2010, during his time at the university, he registered a YouTube account under the name PewDiePie. The following year, he dropped out of Chalmers after losing interest in his degree field, much to the dismay of his parents. After failing to earn an apprenticeship with an advertising agency in Scandinavia, he then focused on creating content for his YouTube channel. To fund his videos, Kjellberg began selling prints of his Photoshop art projects and worked at a hot dog stand. Kjellberg soon gathered a rapidly increasing online following, and in July 2012, his channel surpassed one million subscribers."

Pewdiepie has been posting videos to YouTube for nine years and has undoubtedly earned his godlike number of followers through sheer work and stickability. Imagine just how good you would be at Assassin's Creed: Odyssey if you played it every day for nine years. Actually, it takes a leisurely completionist about 200 hours to finish Odyssey so it doesn't have the scope for that kind of time and effort investment.

But will Kassandra's martial abilities seem to outstrip Pewdiepie's YouTubing abilities by many levels of divinity? Will she seem like a goddess to his celebrity? Yes, it will certainly look that way while you're inside the game. Pewdiepie might have been able to attract 89 million viewers, but a maxed-out Kassandra has the power to murder anyone and anything in the ancient Greek world of Odyssey.

> RPGS. A CLEAR PATH TO DIVINITY

That's why RPGs are so powerful. They enable us to claw our way up from mere mortal to demigod like an intern ascending the hierarchy of some divine global corporation. If we do what we're told and achieve the performance targets, we shall ascend to the godlike status of an executive.

The RPG system recognizes that we want to transcend our mortal frailties and anxieties, that we want to feel godlike. And most importantly, it lays out a clear and achievable path to get there.

Quests.

Leveling.

Gear Upgrades.

Unlockable Abilities.

These are what I call the Four Pillars of Divinity. They support the aqueduct upon which you travel from mortal to demigod, from being an unknown peasant to the very center of a virtual world. Because, just like 89 million people are watching Pewdiepie, every single virtual inhabitant in Odyssey's ancient Greece is there to react to you. The player.

```
Massive Attention + Exceptional Abilities =
                  Godlike
```

And we don't have to struggle away for twenty years to become an executive in Divinity Corporation. We need not work for ten years to become a YouTube sensation. In fact, in neither of those cases is the result even guaranteed. Shit happens. Twenty years at a corporation could just lead to a modest redundancy package after a Limited AI takes over your number-crunching gig. Ten years of YouTubing effort might only lead to 20,000 views per day, earning you $1000 per month. That's not to be sneezed at, but it's not godlike.

We only need to invest 200 hours into Assassin's Creed: Odyssey to immerse ourselves in a godlike experience. No, we won't be godlike when we switch off the game, but at least we've had a taste.

> THE JOURNEY FROM MORTAL TO DEMIGOD

Why is it we find RPGs so satisfying if we're just following someone else's directions to a place of fictional godliness?

Let's be honest. Not all of us are comfortable with the prospect of failure. Yes, we're told that we'll succeed if we 'just keep getting up' after those knockdowns. But that's not always true. We might work our guts out, achieve a morsel of success, and then die of cancer. That's life. You might achieve your dreams. You might reach godlike status like Pewdiepie or Chris Hemsworth. Or you might not. Life has no guarantees.

RPGs *do* come with guarantees. You will max out your character if you put in the effort to do so. You will reach godlike status within the game world if you put in the time. You will get to sip from the chalice of divinity, and all we ask in return is 200 hours of your life.

An RPG is a place where you can work hard, enjoy your work, and know that you will receive the fruits of your labors.

The RPG is the journey and the destination. That's why I keep going there, and I suspect that's why you go there too. That's why we love RPGs.

> Enjoyable Effort + Guaranteed Achievements = Godlike

> CLOSING THOUGHTS FOR THIS CHAPTER

Whether or not my Theory of Godliness resonates with you, my aim is to illustrate a vital part of the narrative designer's mindset.

Curiosity.

Curiosity is the underpinning motivation for most writers, especially science fiction writers. "What if?" is the question that drives the entire science fiction genre.

But with narrative design, your curiosity needs to be more targeted. You need to have an ongoing fascination with gamers. What they want. How they think. Why they love some games and are decidedly 'meh' about others. Why they will do one thing in this context but the polar opposite in another. You have to be prepared to play celebrated games to see what all the fuss is about, or at least feel compelled to watch a few 'Let's Play' videos on YouTube. And you should be reading up on gamer psychology whenever the opportunity presents itself.

In many respects, the narrative designer is a bizarre chimera of writer, behavioral psychologist and sociologist striving to understand this weird and wonderful subculture that is Gaming.

As aforementioned, have a read of Jamie Madigan's book, Getting Gamers. After that, take a good look through the articles over at Quantic Foundry. Nick Yee, author of The Proteus Paradox, is making it his life's work to understand how gamers tick.

And you can always go to the 'horse's mouth', as it were. Be part of the community forums of a few of your favorite games. See what gamers are talking about. Play the 'observational psychologist' for a bit. You'll be amazed by what you can learn by sitting quietly in the corner listening and taking notes.

NARRATIVE DESIGN PROCESS_

> HOW DO YOU CONSTRUCT A STORY EXPERIENCE?

> WHAT GOES INTO A NARRATIVE STRATEGY?

> WHAT IS PROCEDURAL NARRATIVE AND HOW DOES IT WORK?

NARRATIVE BITS_

Now here's a crazy concept to help get those neural pathways growing and tangling into ever denser knots.

Narrative Bits.
'Narbs', for short.

A 'bit' is the smallest unit of data in a computer. It's a 0 or a 1. On its own, it means next to nothing. 0 = off. 1 = on. What is it that's being turned off and on? How does this offing and oning affect me and the world around me? No idea. But when you put billions of 0s and 1s together, you get Grand Theft Auto V which, in 2018, was considered the largest open world game in existence.

So by logical extrapolation, a 'narrative bit' is the smallest possible unit of story. A zero is a narrative bit because it has a meaning. It means, literally, nothing. A one is also a narrative bit because it also means something. It tells the story of being one more than nothing.

> NARBS IN SOCIAL MEDIA

"Narbs" as a term was first coined by Professor Ananda Mitra and his team at Wake Forest University in 2010, and their focus was on social media.

September 11, Al-Qaeda, and New York are by themselves simply a date and two names. Almost meaningless without context. But add those three narbs together and you have a terrifying event that shook the world.

By creating a collage of narbs, Mitra was about to form profiles of social media users. By gathering together someone's comments, photos, and link clicks, you may intuit their food, pets, fashion and sexual preferences. Perhaps you can predict the type of people they are likely to associate with, their political and religious leanings. You could learn that they're an employee of a large corporation or a freelancer, a gamer or a fitness freak, a fashionista or a trekkie, a neo-nazi or an environmentalist. By collating all the little pieces of story we leave behind on the internet, all the narbs, people like Mitra can form an entire story. A person's story.

Yes, this is exactly what Cambridge Analytica did, if you were abreast of that certain internet privacy scandal. By gathering up people's narbs, they could accurately target American voters who were 'on the fence' between Democrat and Republican, and could 'tell them a story' through Facebook advertising that would tip them over the edge.

> NARBS IN GAME OF THRONES

Spoiler Alert!
If you haven't yet watched Game of Thrones, skip to the next section.

Let's start with character action. All the little bits of action, all of those narbs, inform us of who a character is and who they might become.

The Hound.

Sandor Clegane.

Personally, he's my favorite character from GoT because he's wonderfully contradictory. His face is badly scarred by burns. He tells the story of how his own brother, Gregor, pressed his face into the flames for playing with his toy. Although normally a ruthless killer, he flees at the Battle of the Blackwater because everything around him is aflame. He's almost defeated by Beric Dondarrion because Beric wields a flaming sword. He wears a red cloak, the color of fire, because he's a vassal of House Lannister. He is driven by his anger. It 'burns' within him.

 "It's my damn luck I end up with a band of fire worshippers." - Sandor Clegane

The list of narbs goes on right through all eight seasons of GoT. Sandor's fearful relationship with fire is built, bit by bit, until it culminates in a satisfyingly infernal way.

The mise-en-scene in Game of Thrones is also a spectacular use of narbs. You need go no further than House Stark to see a collection of small narrative pieces come together to create a powerful story.

Their castle is called "Winterfell".

Their slogan is "Winter is coming."

Their soldiers wear blue, the color normally associated with anything cold.

Their cloaks are usually trimmed with fur, and their sigil is a fur-clad dire wolf.

"Stark" means "strong" in German, but the word, stark, is also strongly associated with cold climates. In English, stark means "severe" or "bare", and it's no coincidence that winters are often referred to as "severe" and winter is associated with "bare" deciduous trees and frosted ground where the cold stunts grass growth. And through color, the Starks are bound to The Wall and the frigid lands beyond. The wall itself is white and blue, being formed of ice. Even the eyes of the White Walker are blue.

Just like Sandor's narbs associate him with fire and heat, the Starks' narbs associate them with ice and cold.

Through little narbs of action, dialogue and mise-en-scene, Game of Thrones builds its characters and its noble houses bit by narrative bit. And the whole seems larger than the sum of its parts.

> NARBS IN VIDEOS GAMES

In-game storytelling is still young. Donkey Kong, released in 1981, is considered as the first game to tell a story. And it's a rudimentary one.

Donkey Kong kidnaps Mario's girlfriend, Pauline.

Donkey Kong smiles when Mario dies. Not too shabby considering the graphics tech in the 80s.

Pauline has a pink dress and long hair (Princess iconography) and yells "HELP!" in speech balloons.

That's the full sum of storytelling in Donkey Kong.

Compare this to 80s TV storytelling. The Greatest American Hero, Hill Street Blues, Dynasty, The Smurfs and Danger Mouse all started in 1981. That gives you a good idea of the relative maturity of video games versus television in terms of storytelling back then. As of writing this, we've only been telling stories in games for thirty-eight years!

Now that the games industry is producing rich narrative tales like The Last of Us, The Walking Dead and Witcher 3, it's safe to say that we've done a pretty good 'catch up' job. Yet while those three titles showcase the heights of video game storytelling, they are still mainly linear and lean on cinematics to do the narrative heavy lifting. Cinematics require the player to stop playing, sit back and be told a story for a little while. This goes against the very purpose of a video game. It's an interactive medium.

It's better if we don't have to stop playing at all. And no, I don't count the times in Witcher 3 and Alan Wake where you 'walk and talk' with a character within a confined game space. The only difference between a walk-and-talk cutscene and a classic cinematic is that you, the player, can still choose what to look at where to move within narrow limits. Other than that, all interactivity is temporarily shut off.

Narrative bits can ensure a consistently interactive experience. Narbs can be absorbed and digested with minimal interference to the gameplay. They can be pieced together, their full meanings becoming apparent as they are placed in context with other narbs.

Remember, I spoke about 'The Story Experience' back in section one? Here's how narbs can be used to create a story experience.

Warning, another spoiler alert!

Bioshock Infinite was a step in the right direction for experiential storytelling. It uses various types of narbs to establish an atmosphere of religious zealotry and prejudice.

 "God forgives everything. But I'm just a prophet, so I don't have to." - Zachary H. Comstock

This is a piece of ambient dialogue, a voice-over that you hear as you move through an early area in the game. You have full interactive freedom at the point of hearing it, although you don't have a gun yet, so there's no chance of you missing it during a cacophony of gunfire.

In one line the arch-villain, Comstock, establishes his fundamental hypocrisy. He's built a city, Columbia, on the joint principles of 'righteousness' and 'selfishness'. And this attitude is reflected in all the ambient dialogue throughout Columbia.

As you pass by, NPCs express their reverence for God and Comstock while succinctly expressing their condescension of women and their distaste for African-Americans, the Irish, Native Americans and anyone else who cannot live up to their middle-class, Anglo-Saxon ideals. Most dialogue places automatically as you breach an NPCs 'personal bubble'. It's seldom over two lines long, and if you miss... you miss it. You can listen or you can move on. It's up to you.

The Columbia Raffle Fair is a beautifully sinister example of narbs at work. On the surface, the fair is 'delightful', a wonder of 19th diversion for the privileged classes. In particular, there's a shooting gallery, a mini-game where you use an airgun to shoot 'Vox Populi' revolutionaries. You shoot pop-up parodies of people like 'ducks in a row' at a classic sideshow stall. In this singular experience, you are literally interacting with Columbia's dehumanization of their cultural underclasses.

And in many respects, the airgun mini-game foreshadows the extensive use of environmental narbs in the larger shooting gallery that is Bioshock Infinite.

Statues, flags and symbology reinforce the adoration of God, Comstock, George Washington, and the supremacy of the Anglo-American. The household of the Order of the Raven is rich with the imagery of white supremacy, from a rug emblazoned with the slogan 'Protecting Our Race', to large oil paintings that demonize Abraham Lincoln.

The clean, beautiful, light-filled upper levels of Anglo-American Columbia contrast with the grimy, poverty-stricken lower levels where the Blacks, Irish and Chinese live.

The automaton 'Patriots' that you battle against come in two flavors. George Washington for 'white' Columbia. Abraham Lincoln for the Vox Populi.

The racial divisions are even color coded, just like the Starks and the Lannisters in Game of Thrones. This time it's blue and white for Columbia's police and military, and red and black for the Vox Populi revolutionaries.

Every element of the mise-en-scene in Bioshock Infinite reinforces the themes of racial division and cultural zealotry. And it comes from both sides, too. They paint privileged oppressors and uprising underdogs with equally unflattering brushes.

Bioshock Infinite isn't a 'story' about the 'haves' and the 'have nots'. Through the use of narbs it becomes a story experience of social inequality and conflict.

> WHERE TO NEXT WITH NARBS?

Narbs are only as powerful as the writer who designs them. You, as a narrative designer, can learn to apply jigsaw storytelling to your game world, scattering narbs for players to discover. Your players can witness and collect these narbs, absorb their isolated messages, and piece them all together to create a larger meaning and greater understanding.

Bit by bit, narb by narb, they create their own overarching narrative from their interpretations and their moments of epiphany. Their understanding will differ depending on how much they notice, and how much they want to engage with the story experience. Some elements you can make obvious, like the airgun mini-game in Bioshock Infinite. Others, like Columbia's many cutscene-style zoetropes, could be missed or ignored altogether. That doesn't matter. They're there for players who want to deepen their understanding of the game world, but they never impede players who just want to shoot a lot of baddies.

In theory, once a player has gathered and combined all the puzzle pieces, they should come to the same conclusion as any other completionist player. The narbs should add up to a single 'Big Picture' of the story experience. Each player will have reached that jigsaw puzzle image through a different sequence, a different series of insights and epiphanies, a different path to understanding. It's a personalized journey, but one that reaches the same conclusion. But as we know with humanity, no two people ever see exactly the same picture.

Narbs empower us, as game narrative designers, to embrace and create 'story experiences'. We can create a narrative that our players can genuinely play with. Gameplay is about activity, experience, learning and achievement. There's no reason our game stories shouldn't be the same.

DESIGNING A STORY EXPERIENCE
FOR A PLATFORMER GAME_

Now that you're armed with concepts like story experience and narbs, let's look how you might apply these principles to a narrative design. We'll try a classic old platformer game, something an Indie studio might produce for a niche game market.

Platformers can benefit from a story just as much as any other genre. There has to be a reason for all that jumping and whacking, right? So let's start with the most obvious but often overlooked tool in the platformer storytelling arsenal.

> PLAYER CHARACTER

Jumpman was the original incarnation of the now ultra-famous Mario. This was in 1981 in Donkey Kong. Jumpman was a carpenter. He had a pet ape named Donkey Kong who Jumpman supposedly abused. Let's not linger on that rather sordid fact, shall we? Anyway, rather than calling the SPCA, Donkey Kong kidnaps Jumpman's girlfriend, originally named 'The Lady', and jumping, barrel-rolling hilarity ensues.

You could get away with that in 1981. We gamers were still

making human sacrifices to the digital gods in thanks for the mere existence of video games. Now? Different story.

If the game developer's current character description is something like 'just some dude with a big gun' then they are short-changing their number one asset, and that's something a narrative designer really needs to point out.

Is Duke Nukem just some dude with a big gun? Is Sonic the Hedgehog a 'random spiky rodent'? Actually no, he's not a rodent at all. Hedgehogs belong to the shrew species.

Platformer player characters are a central narb in the game and therefore well worth putting time and effort into. They're the one game asset a player will see pretty much all the time. Unlike in a FPS or strategy game, the player character is center stage. Such is the nature of platformers.

So how do we make the most of our player character in story terms?

- Reactive Dialogue
- Emotes
- Visual Evolution

Before we get into these specifics, we'd better first make a player character.

⊏⎯⎯⊐

Her name is Blink. Actually, her real name is Edwina Snodgrass. People call her Blink because she has a strange ability, but mostly because her name is Edwina Snodgrass.

Blink can 'blink' out of existence for a moment, becoming insubstantial, a talent that allows her to walk through walls. However, this power of hers has its downsides. For one, it's illegal within the oppressive nation state she was born into. Second, as a child, she wasn't able to control it very well so ended up in some horrible situations. As a result, she harbors a ton of anxiety around her super power. It really stresses her out, and she's reluctant to use it. Blink never wanted to be a superhero and still doesn't think of herself in those terms.

> NARRATIVE TECHNIQUE. REACTIVE DIALOGUE

This is when you have pieces of dialogue that play in response to in-game events or are triggered when the player character (PC) encounters a specific piece of environment. It was Bastion that first got me thinking about this technique, as it was a nice touch to have that gravelly voiced narrator commentating on the in-game action. It really helped with the sense of immersion and the feeling that player agency was being recognized by the game.

It's also a great example of narbs at work. Each bit of dialogue sits in isolation, waiting to be heard. If the PC doesn't pass through the area, doesn't trigger the dialogue, then the player won't hear it. Each dialogue must be self-contained. A meaningful bit of story in its own right. And these dialogue fragments need to be playable in any order. Together they'll add up to a full story, but there can't be any reliance on a linear sequence (like in a movie) because players have a terrible habit of being non-linear in their play behavior.

Here are two off-the-top-of-my-head examples of reactive dialogues for our Blink platformer.

Event 1: After blinking through a wall, Blink says, "It's like I don't even exist." This is not a good thing for Blink. It's fuel for her existential crisis.

Event 2: After killing a Regime Captain, Blink remarks, "We're the same. Can't you see that?" She can't believe that one human can oppress another. Aren't all humans 'good' deep down?

These dialogues could be done as text bubbles or as voice overs, depending on the developer's budget. And it would pay to have lots of variations for individual events. The player will tire of those lines if they're repeated too often. In fact, it might be best to save them for special events and unique mobs, but it all comes down to the gameplay. As a narrative designer, it's always good to do a playthrough to see if the reactive dialogues are getting distracting or tiresome.

Reactive dialogue is also great for showing off character development. What if, by Level 5, Blink is coming to terms with her super hero status and is getting quite fired up about her one-woman rebellion against the regime?

Event 1: After blinking through a wall, Blink growls, "Like a vengeful spirit." There's a sense of aggressive purpose to her now.

Event 2: After killing a Regime Officer, Blink shouts, "Just doing your job? Yeah, me too!" Ooh, getting a little bitter there, Blink.

Blink is shedding her anxiety in favor of a growing confidence and sense of empowerment, but there's a scary edge to her now. Is she starting to lose touch with her own humanity? Let's hope not! Uh oh, look what's on her mind at Level 10!

Event 1: After blinking through a wall, Blink declares, "I am the chosen one." God complex!

Event 2: When facing her boss fight with the Regime General, Blink remarks, "Since you did such a bad job of running this country, how about you let me have a go?" Is Blink becoming the one thing she despises most? Is she the next tyrant?

As you can see, there's a lot that can be done for character development with just a few lines of dialogue, and there's no need to push for the forking out of great wads of cash on voice actors. Text is often all you need to get the point across.

———

Although it's not a platformer, let's take a quick look at Darkest Dungeon. Aside from their now legendary narrator, all of their in-game dialogue is delivered in text boxes. As long as the lines are short and sharp, and presented when the player has a moment or two to absorb them, they'll have the desired effect.

Actually, that brings me to the most important point about Reactive Dialogue.

Timing.

By their very nature, platformers are high-action beasties, but they have their quiet moments. You don't want to present dialogue whilst the player is trying to jump Blink to that fast-moving platform which has been cunningly suspended over an acid pool filled with mutant, acid-resistant piranhas. Nor is there any point in asking the player to read while Blink is fending off a wave of jack-booted regime stormtroopers.

If Blink is standing safely on the platform, or has finished off the last stormtrooper, then it's a good time to present a speech bubble. In the breathing spaces between the jump-fests and frenetic whacking sessions, moments of character reflection can be poignant.

And no, it's not weird that Blink is talking to herself. Duke Nukem talks to himself all the time, and he's no weirdo... right?

Now, before we wrap this up, I will offer you up a little table that you might want to use when writing up your Reactive Dialogue.

Blink Reactive Dialogue_ Game Level 1_ Streets of Grim			
Line No.	Trigger	Tone	Dialogue [120 Character Limit]
1.0	First use of Blink in Level 1	Unsettled	It's like I don't even exist.
1.1	Death of Captain	Bewildered	We're the same. Can't you see that?
1.2	Death of Captain	Troubled	???
1.3	Death of Captain	Remorseful	???

The line numbers are useful for the level designer who will implement this text within the game. It means they can tell the game engine to "show line 1.1 in the player character text" when "the blink power is activated for the first time". Numbering your dialogue lines is also a good habit to get into for voice recording.

It's also great to provide the emotional context for each line of dialogue so that an animator can reinforce that emotion with a player character expression. An 'emote' which we'll talk about next. Once again, statements of emotional context such as "unsettled" are also helpful to voice actors.

> NARRATIVE TECHNIQUE. EMOTES

Are we talking about Emojis? Smiley face, sad face, lol, facepalm?! Yes and no. Emojis are a subset of emotes. With emotes, we're looking at the bigger animal kingdom of 'symbols that can represent human emotion'.

And yes, emotes are narbs. Tiny bits of narrative expression that can add up to something big and meaningful.

To clarify, we're not considering the text and verbalized emotes that one finds in games like Hearthstone. "Thanks",

"Wow", "Oops", "Well Played", "Greetings" and the obtuse "Threaten". Horribly generic and a clumsy way to circumvent PvP abuse. I don't consider them to be emotes at all. They're more like Remarks, a replacement for PC dialogue, and not very good ones at that. Emotes are a symbolic representation of an emotion. A one hit wonder of expressed feeling. They can be as simple as a question or exclamation mark in a thought bubble, or they can be an enthusiastic 'sky punch' like one sees Hopper do in the Stranger Things RPG when he scores a security card. They're our shorthand language for expressing our player character's personality, a way to build the illusion that sprites are people too!

Let's say we have the art and animation budget to create a range of expressions for our supergirl player character, Blink. Should we start with facial expressions or go for full-body expressions? That totally depends on how big our player character is compared to the rest of the screen, and whether we're creating for big screens (console and PC) or little screens (mobile). Let's look at both options for a minute. Technical considerations are just another element, along with game mechanics, that a narrative designer needs to take into account when planning a story.

> BIG SCREEN EMOTES

If we only need to cater for big screens then it's possible for us to do facial expressions. Now, being a writer, not an illustrator, I won't go into the finer points of cartoon expressions. But thanks to emoticons, we've been schooled in symbolic face design since Dr. Scott Fahlman invented the first ":-)" in 1982. The first graphical emoji wasn't created until seventeen years later, by Shigetaka Kurita.

And we need not create the Mona Lisa for every occasion here. You need go no further than The Order of the Stick to see how much subtlety can be squeezed out of a circle, a few well-placed lines and some shading.

> SMALL SCREEN EMOTES

While we might get away with facial expressions on most full-sized tablets, things get pokey and obscure on anything from an iPad Mini downwards. But that's okay. We still have a few options. The first is to employ the whole body in our emotional expression. Yes, I'm talking about Hopper's sky punches again.

- Poses
- Arm gestures
- Little dances
- Slumped or slouched posture
- Short steps or long steps
- Shuffling or marching

These are all ways to convey feelings without the need for anything as discernable as an actual 'face'.

Depending on the style of the platformer you're working with, you can go even more symbolic. You can abstract the player character's inner workings using thought bubbles and basic pictograms. The Scary Girl platformer does a superb job of this, conveying some quite complex concepts through sequences of pictograms. Machinarium takes this one step further by playing mini-animations within thought bubbles to represent the PC's inner world.

Another option is to feature a profile pic of your PC in a thought bubble or some other little container that lets the player know it's referring to inner world stuff, not outer world stuff. These profile pics can be created to express a range of emotions, essentially as 'selfies' of the player character's feelings. This is a technique that's quite common in visual novels. For the creation of our Falconers visual novel, Moonlight, we had our artist draw six different headshots for the PC and each main NPC in the story.

- Neutral
- Contemplative (Eyes closed, mouth open)
- Happy
- Surprised
- Angry
- Sad

When combined with other elements, such as text and environment, it's amazing how many subtle emotions can be drawn out based on the context. An Angry profile pic can also be used for Frustrated, Disgusted, Intimidating, Determined and Insulted, to name but a few. Think about how a scowl can be used in response to either a pointed finger or a hapless shrug. Same expression, but quite a different emotional interpretation because of the difference in context.

> THE BASICS

The above approaches can get a bit art-heavy, so it really depends on the game's art team and budget. If they're running on the smell of an oily paint brush, then there's nothing wrong with falling back on the basics.

:-|

:-\

:-)

:-o

x-(

:-(

?

!

Honestly, something is better than nothing when adding emotional nuances to your player character. As you add an emote, your PC instantly has an inner world that's separate from your player. They have their own thoughts and feelings, their own ways of reacting to the game world. That's what makes them a Character rather than an Avatar.

> BLINK HAS FEELINGS TOO

Before we wrap this section up, let's see some basic emote design with Supergirl Blink. We'll use the same basic planning principles as we used with reactive dialogue because emotes should always be an emotional reaction to an event or piece of game world. They don't work well in isolation.

Blink Reactive Dialogue_ Game Level 1_ Streets of Grim			
Emote No.	Trigger	Emotion	Symbol
1.0	First use of Blink in Level 1	Unsettled	Expression = :-| Body language = Hugs herself or folds her arms as an act of self protection.
1.1	Death of Captain	Bewildered	Expression = :-(Body language = Hunched, shaking head, hands outstretched with palms up.
1.2	Death of Captain	Troubled	Expression = :-o Body language = Taking a step backwards, hands pressed to her mouth.
1.3	Death of Captain	Remorseful	Expression = :-(Body language = Hands in pockets, head bowed, smaller steps as she walks.

> NARRATIVE TECHNIQUE. VISUAL EVOLUTION

Visual Evolution is just a fancy way of saying that your plat-forming player character is changing before your eyes as you progress through the game. And that exterior change should reflect their interior change.

The simplest and most obvious versions of this in loot-based ARPGs like Path of Exile and Grim Dawn. As the player progresses through the game, they pick up equipment. When items are equipped to their PC, their on-screen appearance changes. The stronger the character grows, the better loot drops they can access, leading to a much more impressive 'look' for the PC as they are equipped with increasingly epic gear. The player character's inner strength, their Level and Stats, are directly reflected in their outer strength through the gear they strut about in. But what if you want to express something more subtle than how heroic and epic your player character is becoming? Well, gear can come to the party here, too.

> GEAR AS CHARACTER

Yes, in-game items are narbs, and a platformer can make use of these narbs just as easily as an ARPG can. In Dan the Man, the premium version offers a customizable player character, but instead of picking up new costume elements for their player character during the game, the player can earn money that can be used to purchase new pieces of costume. This is great if you love dressing up dolls but not so good if you want to show character progression through costume.

So let's build on the Dan the Man example. We could curate the bits of costume and gear that a player can pick up in such a way that it reflects deeper changes in their PC.

There's an interesting psychological effect called 'Enclothed Cognition' that goes on here. No need to go into the studies and details. Suffice to say that what we wear has a direct influence on how we behave. After putting on a police uniform, people feel a little more authoritative. After putting on a lab coat, people feel a little 'smarter'. Try it for the next couple of days. Go out all in black on one day, then on the following day, go out in bright colors. Note the differences in how you behave each day and you might be a tad surprised.

The Enclothed Cognition effect also translates into virtual

worlds. Best if we use our reluctant super-girl, Blink, as our model to demonstrate.

> BLINK PHASE 1. CONFIDENCE AND POWER

At the beginning of our platformer, Blink is dressed in drab greys and blues. Her outfit is shapeless and baggy. She doesn't feel comfortable in her own skin, so she hides her body and tries to fade into the background. But once Blink has completed the first couple of levels and kicked some fascist ass, we offer her collectable outfits that not only have performance buffs like '20% increased movement speed', they are also more form-fitting and come in power-oriented colours like black and red.

Will these snazzy new outfits encourage the player to play more confidently, perhaps take a few more risks? According to the psychologists, yes they will.

So far we've just done the usual ARPG thing, offered gear that empowers the PC. Now let's try something a little different.

> BLINK PHASE 2. MORAL AMBIGUITY

During the next few levels, as Blink goes deeper into regime territory and overcomes increasingly tough odds, we offer items with powerful buffs and some unsettling aesthetics. Since Blink is picking up gear from fallen regime hench-persons, she starts to look like she belongs to the regime. Will this subtly encourage the player to be more ruthless, a little less empathetic in their choices? Creepily... yes.

> BLINK PHASE 3. TURNING POINT

What a coincidence! Blink happens upon stockpiles of confiscated items in the higher levels of the game. They once belonged to freedom fighters, like herself, who were captured and executed for their transgressions. Now Blink has the option of a makeover. She can continue to develop her 'regime look', and take advantage of a steady ascendancy of buffs, or she can switch to the brightly colored outfits of her predecessors, yet have to deal with some pretty idiosyncratic stat combos.

We're offering the player an interesting emotional choice. The predictability and cognitive comfort of the dark path versus the challenging and often OTT path of light. Or perhaps some 'shadow rainbow' combination of the two?

> FLESH AND BLOOD CHANGES

Remember Doom? Do you recall how the little profile picture looked steadily more 'beat up' the lower the player character's health got? Seeing my PC in a sorry state motivated me to find a health pack and be very careful until I did. It was far more effective than any health bar or number display. That bloodied face helped me really feel the punishment my PC was taking.

You could do this with a platformer PC. The lower their health, the sicker they look. Once health is restored, they look like a box of birds. There's no need to reflect these states in the mechanics, unless you really want to. The visuals are enough to strengthen the empathic connection between player and PC.

Let's try this from a different angle. What if Blink were to look increasingly athletic as she progresses through the levels, to show the sheer physical exertion and development she's experiencing?

Or, what if her blink power has a side effect? The more she uses it, the more insubstantial she starts to look, like she's becoming less and less anchored in the real world?

The art team could just make the Blink PC increasingly translucent or pale, depending how it worked with the scenery. Just the fact that Blink is starting to look like her own ghost, that's enough to give the player's spine a tingle.

> VISUAL CHARACTER ARC

With both Gear and Flesh, we're talking about creating a visual character arc for the platformer's player character, an in-your-face reminder that the PC is growing and changing in response to the journey within the game. There are more ways to do this than I've laid out here, but at least we're thinking in some fresh directions.

And that's really what this whole section about platformer design has been about, to offer you an insight into how the narrative design process looks when it's put into action. As you might have noticed, there's a pretty broad definition of 'writing' going on here. Writing and experience design tend to blend more and more the deeper you go into narrative design.

Don't worry. That's something you'll get used to. ;-P

THE NARRATIVE STRATEGY_

Smart game devs bring a narrative designer in at the very beginning of the development process. When this happens, it's the ND's job to come up with a sound narrative strategy for their game. This is the ND's opportunity to make the game mechanics and narrative sing in near perfect ludo narrative harmony.

> WHAT IS A NARRATIVE STRATEGY?

It's a document that lays out the fundamental story experience the game wants to deliver and the nuts and bolts of how that story experience will be realised.

A good narrative strategy starts with lore and characters, strongly establishing the world that the player will explore and interact with. But it shouldn't go into the nitty gritty of that lore. Land history, character profiles, divine pantheons, creation stories... that stuff all goes into a specific lore document. And it's not a storyline document either. It's not here to lay out the plot arcs and quest lines. A narrative strategy document summarizes the most important elements of our game story and then focuses on how to implement those elements.

> A SIDE NOTE ON LORE

Lore can be a trap. I've seen too many NDs get bogged down in epic creation stories and the forging of extensive pantheons, 'stirring stuff' that ends up having very little impact on the game world. The player doesn't care what happened 10,000 years ago when the Dragon of Light ate the Salmon of Knowledge and sat down to excrete the Land of Nod. Not unless it has a direct impact on their gameplay.

Is the Dragon of Light a big boss they can fight at some point?

Are there bits of the Salmon of Knowledge still sitting about as yummy caches of experience points?

If not, save all that high level lore for the other end of the narrative design process, when you're doing the lore tomes and general 'points of interest'. For now, focus only on the lore that the player truly needs. Lore that helps them understand what to do in this game world.

> EXAMPLE: A DARK FANTASY ARPG (ACTION ROLEPLAYING GAME)

You're tasked with creating the narrative for a dark fantasy ARPG called Demon Days, inspired by the Gorillaz song of the same name.

This is a slaughterhouse of a game where the players will grind their way through thousands of demonic mobs. Their player character will grow ever more powerful and epic until they reach 'godlike' status and save the world. It's for fans of games like Diablo 3, Path of Exile and Grim Dawn.

These are the two most important questions you need to ask

about the Demon Days game story and how it relates to the players.

1. What do you want your players to know?
2. What do you want your players to WANT to know?

> PLEASING THE MAJORITY

The following strategy will focus on Midcore Players. Since they form most of the ARPG player base, they are the ones who provide the financial foundation for a game like Demon Days.

Yes, there's a lot of talk around the games industry about 'hunting whales', that tiny minority of players who will spend small fortunes on your game. I'm not a fan of this strategy. It feels callous and exploitative. And you don't have to look far to find cases where gamers have gone into serious debt to make in-app purchases in their favorite video games. I prefer the "reasonable taxation" method that keeps most democratic nations afloat. A little bit from many people goes a long way. Whether your game is premium or freemium, Midcore Players can form the economic powerhouse that keeps you and your fellow devs making games in perpetuity... if you treat them well.

> THE THREE BEARS

Keeping with this whole 'Goldilocks' theme, I've developed the 'Three Bears' approach to help get the narrative elements 'just right' for Midcore Players. And for this exercise, I'll abbreviate Demon Days to "DD".

Let's introduce you to the three bears.

1. Mama Bear: Lore that rewards the player with concrete Gameplay payoffs.
2. Papa Bear: Lore that builds understanding of the characters the player will meet and/or fight in-game.
3. Baby Bear: Lore that provides clues to the unravelling of an overarching mystery.

> MAMA BEAR. LORE MEETS GAMEPLAY

In DD we have several options for touch points between Lore and Gameplay.

A: Quests

- Demon Research quests
- History Research quests

B: Consumable Items
C: Weapons and Armor

Quests
Delivery: In DD, quests are usually offered by an NPC (Non-player Character) through dialogue or text (depending on the development budget).

Payoff: By completing quests, players explore the world and game mechanics in a goal-oriented way that Midcore Players tend to find satisfying.

Quests can also offer experience points and stat improvements for their character, serving up some concrete rewards for completing what is ostensibly an interactive short story.

For a good example of a quest with concrete rewards, look back at the Lords of Larceny quest from Path of Exile. Not only does the quest offer an opportunity to harvest a lot of experience points and loot from mobs, each bandit lord (or lady) provides a permanent passive buff once the player has handed over all three pieces of the pyramid. The buff varies, depending which bandit takes possession of the quest item, so players can choose whether to complete the quest out of pragmatism, going for the stat improvement that best suits their character build, or go with a more story-focused approach where the work for the NPC whose perspective they agree with. When designing the Lords of Larceny quest, I ensured that the four opposing NPCs (Eramir, Kraityn, Avira and Oak) each have differing views of how exiles can survive and thrive in the post-apocalyptic world of Wraeclast. The player can side with the perspective they most agree with or with the character they like best.

When designing quests for Midcore Players, it's important to balance the practical with the emotional. The concrete payoff should be worth it, but as seen in the Witcher 3 quest where Geralt helps an old lady get her favorite pan back, sometimes a fun interaction with an interesting character is enough.

Narrative Strategy Style

Okay, let's get into the nitty gritty of this narrative strategy example. The following sections lay out various story experience approaches for DD, and they're written how I would normally present them in a working document for game developers.

Remember, a narrative strategy is a living, breathing thing. What you see below is what I would start with when designing story experiences for Demon Days. It's a first draft. I would then hand it over to the development team for review and feedback. After that, it's an iteration process that carries on throughout the development of the game. I'd be constantly updating the narrative strategy, adjusting it to fit the mechanics and art of the game as the various elements are built.

It's nearly impossible to predict what the narrative strategy will look like near the end of a game's development, but you've got to start somewhere, so let's dive into this first draft below.

> NARRATIVE STRATEGY 1. MAMA BEAR'S GAMEPLAY REWARDS

Demon Research

These quests will be given primarily by a mad scientist NPC named Vostik. He wants the player to hunt and kill specific demons and collect their body parts so he can research new and effective ways to slaughter said demons. Sometimes, he may want the player to capture live demons for 'experimentation'.

Macabre, right? Well, this is a dark fantasy we're dealing with here.

Demon Research quests are a good opportunity to express the lore surrounding the demons and their origins. A chance for midcores to get to know their enemies, and for lore junkies to immerse themselves in the demon side of our fictional world.

As a mechanical payoff, we'll have Vostik offer the fruits of his research in the form of combat bonuses. Since he'll be able to identify demonic strengths and weaknesses, he'll be able to offer the player combat buffs when fighting demons that the player has already hunted, and perhaps those that are closely related in some way. For instance, by hunting a certain type of Diseased Demon, the player could gain a buff from Vostik that helps them battle all types of Fire demon.

Example Delivery: Through a voice-over, Vostik asks the player to collect the Pathogen Glands of ten Spitslingers.

1. Vostik's delivery dialogue reveals the favored locations and usual behaviors of a Spitslinger.
2. A Pathogen Gland (Quest Item) has flavor text next to the inventory image that gives a little history about the demonic disease these creatures carry.

Example Payoff: Vostik develops a serum that provides a permanent % resistance increase against all disease-related attacks.

NPC arc over multiple quests: Vostik's attitude towards his research will reveal much of his character, his obsessions, his relationship to the demons. The player will eventually discover that Vostik is a rebel demon possessing a human body, and that he wants to help the humans defeat the demons so he can remain free of the cruel demonic overlords.

Quests prompting Gameplay Challenges: Vostik could specify a method of dispatch for certain demon types, such as "use only melee" or "use only magic". The reasoning would be that Vostik needs different portions of a demon body each time, and that certain attacks would damage the specimen while other attacks would preserve it. These challenges could offer bonus XP are a good way to re-use mobs while still offering variation in the combat experience.

Pause for Consideration

Step out of the narrative strategy doc for a moment to consider a couple of things.

First, note how the above quest design hones in on the details of a specific quest while also considering that quest's place in Vostik's overarching subplot.

This is a juggling act that any good narrative design must perform. Questing should have a Gestalt thing happening. They should be fun and satisfying in isolation, but a collection of quests should add up to something greater than the sum of its parts.

In this example, that 'greater' is the revelation that Vostik is actually a demon, and that there's a minority of demonkind who, like Vostik, want to live peacefully and freely. Not all demons are bad guys!

You'll also notice that in the Splitslinger Quest we've audaciously suggested gameplay options to the game design team. How dare we! This is a good example of the mindset shift that must happen when migrating from writer to game designer. In a game development context, a writer is there to react to the mechanics with dialogue and flavor text. But a game designer works with the mechanics, designing moments where the story has a mechanical payoff, and vice versa.

No, a narrative designer need not be a fully fledged game designer. But narrative designer's need to understand the mechanics enough to see how gameplay and story can work together to forge a fun experience for the player.

Okay, let's get back to the narrative strategy.

History Research

These quests will be given primarily by the leader of the human stronghold.

Constance is a cold and calculating woman who sees demon invasion as an opportunity to rise to power in this beleaguered land.

Constance's quests will be about collecting relics and exploring the ruins of the ancient civilization that was devastated by the previous demonic invasion, roughly 1000 years ago. Although Constance never reveals this outright, she hopes the player will uncover lost knowledge and technology that she can use to both defeat the demons and wrest control of the land from the current monarch.

There are several gameplay reward types we could offer the player in return for their lore-hunting efforts.

History Fragments can have the following functions:

1. To inform the player of the world's various environmental hazards and empower them to activate these hazards against enemies. For example: Throwing a Pathogen Gland into a Toxin Pool will generate a Noxious Cloud that damages any demon within the area of effect (AoE). These gameplay hints could take the form of ancient scientific documents.
2. To provide navigational information about the world. Fragments of maps and floor-plans could provide the locations of waypoints and 'places of interest' where ancient technology caches might be found.
3. To provide blueprints for ancient weaponry that could be forged by the stronghold's weaponsmith (Anthea) once all the materials have been gathered.

Example Delivery: Through a voice-over, Constance asks the player to recover a map of Gull's Crag Island from the ruins of the Harbormaster's Office. She hopes the map will reveal the location of the Gull's Crag waypoint, as she hopes to send troops to Gull's Crag and use it as a staging point for her conquest of the docks.

1. In dialogue, Constance briefly explains the history of Gull's Crag as a fortress built to protect the harbor from pirates.
2. The Gull's Crag Map (Quest Item) offers hints that Gull's Crag has a more sinister purpose than simple harbor security. It shows that the old fortress was home to a demonologist's laboratory.

Example Payoff: Possession of the Gull's Crag Map removes the Fog of War over the Gull's Crag area, making the whole location available in the player's HUD map. This means the player doesn't have to manually remove the Fog of War through exploration.

NPC arc over multiple quests: Bit by bit, it becomes apparent that Constance has a nefarious ambition. She doesn't want to rid the land of demons. She wants to control the demons and use them as her personal army. She wants to rule the land as a Demon Queen!

Side Note. Designing for wider appeal: Since lore is typically attractive to solo-player completionists, collecting History Fragments could provide mechanical benefits to PVP engagement in order to incentivize online players to take part.

Items: Weapons and Armor

Items are the lifeblood of ARPGs like Demon Days. Loot drops are a major attraction for fans of this genre. And while the item's mechanics are vital to hardcore players in their quests to optimize their character builds, items can also be a rich source of story for midcores and lore junkies.

Art and flavor text are the two primary methods for conveying Lore through Items. In DD we could effectively break flavor text down into two main types.

1. Self-Contained
2. Jigsaw

Self-Contained Flavor Text offers an insight into a specific piece of the fictional world, but it does not directly connect to any other piece of flavor text. It's a stand-alone narrative element.

e.g. Hallistan's Halberd - "Stab the infected from a distance or become the infected." - Hallistan the Harbinger.

Jigsaw Flavor Text comprises multiple linked flavor texts that form the parts of a whole story. They can be used in association with historical characters, both human and demonic. Each part of a full set of armor and weaponry offers an insight into the past personality and actions of their former owner. When read together, these flavor texts should provide a complete understanding of that character. A full set of these items can be collected and worn, allowing a player to literally 'wear the identity' of that epic character.

The following is a sample set of items from Bloodgate: Age of Alchemy, a dark fantasy Match 3 ARPG (yes, there is such a thing) that I worked on fairly early in my narrative design career. In fact, it was my second only 'big gig' after Path of Exile.

Bloodgate: Age of Alchemy_ Item Sets		
Helmet	Rimewolf's Scalp	"The further a wolf roams, the more it understands." - Eskara Rimewolf
Chestplate	Rimewolf's Heart	"Guard your heart from the hoarfrost of doubt." - Eskara Rimewolf
Gauntlets	Rimewolf's Wards	"Hold strong in your belief and ward off the blows of the ignorant." - Eskara Rimewolf
Leggings	Rimewolf's Stance	"Standing is not a matter of placing your feet. It's a matter of placing yourself." - Eskara Rimewolf
Ring	Rimewolf's Eye	"A wolf knows that one set of eyes is never enough." - Eskara Rimewolf
Amulet	Rimewolf's Totem	"A true wolf never hunts alone." - Eskara Rimewolf

Together, Eskara Rimewolf's flavor texts depict a strong-willed hero who has faced many dangerous challenges and developed a resilient mindset for dealing with those challenges. And it's also clear that he's no 'lone wolf'. He's a team player who understands the power of collective strength.

Mechanical Payoff: We can also have a gameplay reward for the collection of Rimewolf's full set of items. When worn together, that could create a 'synergy buff', and a large percentage bonus in defense against cold attacks. Several keywords have already been put in place to establish Rimewolf's association with the cold climes.

Rime = frost.
Wolf = animal found in cold climates.
Hoarfrost = frozen water vapor.

Resistance to cold is also in thematic harmony with Rimewolf's staunch resilience as a character. His is a quiet strength developed over many years in harsh environments.

> STRATEGY 2. PAPA BEAR'S CHARACTERS

Character is what an audience engages with above all else.

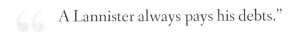 A Lannister always pays his debts."

These are the tools at our disposal for characterisation.

1. What an NPC or Boss says about themselves.
2. What NPCs and Bosses reveal about themselves when they speak of other topics.
3. What others say of an NPC or Boss in dialogue.
4. Story Glyphs (Tomes, Audio Logs…) that reveal the past actions of NPCs and Bosses.
5. Item Flavor Text associated with Bosses.

`Monologues about Self`
It's best to avoid having characters talk about themselves too much.

 I'm the kind of person who…" [shudder].

Example: Vostik.

 I recall little about the one whose body I now inhabit. But I gather from its condition that he undervalued it."

Unless, of course, we want the character to seem self-absorbed. This would be fine for Bosses.

Example: When the player first encounters the demon boss, Flameye.

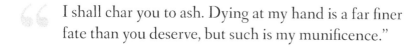

> I shall char you to ash. Dying at my hand is a far finer fate than you deserve, but such is my munificence."

The overall aim is to keep monologues as short and to the point as possible. Midcore Players often skip through dialogue that goes over 10 to 20 seconds.

Monologues about Others

It can be effective to have dialogue options where NPCs voice their opinions about other NPCs in the Hub. If done well, these dialogues produce an illusion of community. This is particularly important in settings like DD where NPCs have been placed in fixed positions and cannot move. Therefore, they will never be heard conversing with each other.

Anthea about Vostik:

> I think it's sort of cute how he lunges out of the shadows and asks me if I need anything."

In this way we integrate attitudes into various dialogue options so that we build up a picture of how one NPC feels about another.

Constance, accepting a Metallurgy Document from a History Quest:

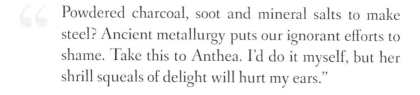

> Powdered charcoal, soot and mineral salts to make steel? Ancient metallurgy puts our ignorant efforts to shame. Take this to Anthea. I'd do it myself, but her shrill squeals of delight will hurt my ears."

Story Glyphs

Since the demons have been around a long time and were instrumental in the destruction of the ancient civilisation that preceded the culture of the player-characters and NPCs, we have the option of seeing these demons through the long-dead eyes. These Story Glyphs could come in the form of Diaries, Communication Documents and Plans regarding the defense of the ancient lands against the demon invasion.

Example: Communication Doc about a demon nest:

Captain Denniston,
The demonic nest in Verdant Common continues to spew forth its aberrations. I've heard it's been dubbed 'The Mother' now. Someone has a warped perception of parenthood. If we don't get fresh munitions to Colonel Carruthers his forces will be overrun, and the capitol soon after. Take as many marines as you need from the docks and apply their labors to the munitions factory.
The people are relying on us.
Signed,
Admiral Forsythe

Flavor Text for Items dropped by Demon Bosses

Since our Demon Bosses will continually respawn, it becomes possible to milk these battles for their narrative content alongside the action.

Each Boss Monster could have a kit of items that can be collected from them, and each item would feature a piece of Jigsaw Flavor Text.

When the PC kills Flameye, the demon boss will drop a special item that's part of his kit. A kit is the sum of items that a monster boss has associated with him.

In the first instance, Flameye will drop his Hellfire Helm.

 A burning soul is a lovely thing
Always it makes me think of spring.
As in my grate it overfills,
And reminds me of incinerating daffodils."

The flavor texts on Flameye's Kit Items will collectively portray his affinity for destruction, fire and bad poetry.

Lore meets Mystery
In Demon Days, we have an overarching mystery that we can gradually unveil over the course of the game. Where did the demons come from?

Misinformation and 'Myth-information'
The human survivors of the first invasion passed on their tragedy via oral storytelling from generation to generation. Over the centuries that followed the invasion, these tales morphed from factual accounts into legends and ultimately into myths. Now the basic myth, perpetuated by the main religious order in DD, is that the demons rose up from Hell to punish humanity for its many sins.

We can use PC and NPC dialogue to relate these tells of damnation and woe. These monologues will be largely apocryphal.

Vostik:

 The time and manner of the world's end had been predicted many times over by scholars, saints, and madmen. None of them got it right, of course, save one lowly hermit whose name is now lost to us. A mob tore him to pieces, certain that his prescience could only result from demonic possession. As a result, the art of prophecy has fallen out of fashion, although I predict a major comeback two weeks hence, after sundown. But don't quote me on that."

Fragmentary Information: The Ancient Ruins

But we don't want any single Story Glyph to lay out exactly how anything happened during the first demonic invasion. Piece by piece, we want the player to build their own pictures and posit their own theories. This part of the Mystery Strategy will tie in very closely to Constance's research quests, although many of these History Fragments could be laid into the ruins to be discovered independently by the player.

Example:

> As I expected, the marble pilasters of Guthwulf's laboratory become hyper conductive when subjected to the considerable heat exerted by...machines...still pinning my leg but I am confident that wit...so hungr...aw rat tastes like chicke...starting a fire to signal for hel...fire sprea...out of cont...urni...liv...ell Lavinia I don't...ove her aft...all..."

Narrative Note: We could develop a small cast of historical characters who have written a series of these fragments each.

Fragmentary Information: The Demons

We could have four main sources for expressing the fragmented history of demons.

1. Monologues from Vostik.
2. Intros and Battle Taunts from Bosses.
3. Item Flavor Text.
4. Dialogue between the player and Vostik.

Monologues from Vostik

Once it is discovered that Vostik is actually a demon inside a human body, a type of 'sentient virus', the player could question him about the origins of other demons. Vostik should never give a straight answer, establishing him as an unreliable narrator.

Example: Vostik, when asked about the origins of demons

 We came from the firmament. Did we do it willingly or were we vomited up? And if we were ejected then who or what ejected us? And why did we agree to go? Why didn't we stick in our maker's craw like so much asphyxiating bile?"

Intros and Battle Taunts from Bosses

There isn't a lot of scope for clue dropping in these short and sharp monologues, but there's room for at least some hints.

Example: The Mother Intro
The Mother:

 You are the weeds I pull from my garden. You humans... seeded with no thought, no purpose. You are an accident!"

Item Flavor Text

Flavor Text in our demon item kits can do double duty for us.

While building up demonic characters, they can also provide insights into the origins of the demons.

Example: Fist of Flameye (Firestorm Gauntlet).

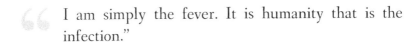 I am simply the fever. It is humanity that is the infection."

Player and Vostik Dialogue, if Vostik is able to accompany the PC:

Through scripted dialogue sequences, the PC could directly question Vostik about the origins of both humans and monsters.

Example 1: Having heard The Mother's introduction and killed her for the first time.

The Mother:

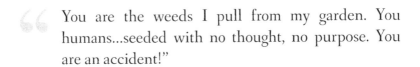 You are the weeds I pull from my garden. You humans...seeded with no thought, no purpose. You are an accident!"

PC:

 Humans are an accident? What did she mean?

Vostik:

 No design.

PC:

What? Of course not. You don't design a baby.

Vostik:

 Then how do you know what sort of offspring you'll spawn?

PC:

 You don't. Wait... were you designed?

Vostik:

 Yes.

PC:

 Who by?

Vostik:

 (sadly) If only I knew.

> FINAL WORDS ON NARRATIVE STRATEGY

There are as many types of narrative strategies as there are genres and subgenres of video games. The above Demon Days strategy is neither a definitive example of an ARPG narrative strategy, nor is it even a complete one.

That's the mercurial nature of video game narrative for you. Every game requires a fresh strategy that accounts for its mechanics, its audience, its themes and its goals. And seldom will two strategies look alike.

Basically, I'm saying that the Demon Days narrative strategy exemplifies a mindset rather than a model. It shows the things you need to consider when developing a specific narrative strategy for a specific game.

But at its heart, the DD strategy strives for ludonarrative harmony, something that every narrative strategy should attempt to achieve. In fact, rather than narrative strategy, we might call it a ludo narrative strategy.

Nah. Sounds a bit too academic for me. ;-P

A FIVE STEP APPROACH TO MAKING MONSTERS_

Following on from the narrative strategy in the previous chapter, let's hone in on what is possibly the most important part of a dark fantasy ARPG.

Monsters!

Dark fantasy ARPGs simply don't work unless you have a sea of creepy mobs and downright horrific bosses to wade through.

In my experience, it's not the narrative designer's job to come up with mob concepts. At least not directly. The level designers will take cues from your world design (hopefully), but generally, you won't have too much say in how the mobs shape up.

In fact, mobs are a good indicator of a narrative designer's role in the dev team. It's up to the ND to provide the broad strokes of the fictional world, and it's down to the level designers and art team to fill in the details.

However, it is the ND's job to come up with the main events in an ARPG, the moments when all that grinding culminates in an epic battle against a terrifying Boss.

While mobs can be considered part of the environment in a

PvE experience, Bosses are characters and therefore fall within the narrative designer's jurisdiction.

Don't want to make ARPGs when you grow up?

Fair enough, too. They're not everyone's cup of steaming blood. You may want to design adorable kitty cats for a feline-theme free-to-play. In that case, the following monster design strategy is still relevant... in principle.

Creature design of any kind is about honing in on the psychology of the players who will interact with these creatures. How do you want them to feel about your English Blue or Ineffable Behemoth? How can your creature design trigger gut reactions in a way that serves rather than disrupts the story experience?

It's no good having cute demons. The player will feel bad about slaughtering them. Just as it's no good creating a monstrous cat for your F2P feline game.

A narrative designer needs to look at a creature design and recognize the psychological cues that may attract, repulse, or simply bore your prospective player.

> BREAKING THE MONSTER MOLD

Orcs, goblins, trolls and gelatinous cubes. These are but a few of the regulars we see prowling the dungeons of our RPGs. Some may find their presence comforting. I find them duller than dishwater and half as useful.

So what do we do if we want to create a monster that's a step beyond the tried-and-true tropes?

I was fortunate enough to attend a talk by Delaney King on "Art Monsters" where she laid out the four fears we should consider when designing a monster.

Fear of Death

- Anything even vaguely associated with corpses and carcasses, skeletons, and anything of a funereal nature like shrouds, coffins and graveyards. FoD can also be extended to any carrion creatures, from maggots to crows, ants to vultures. For example: Zombies.

Fear of Infection

- Or more fundamentally... fear of sickness. This could be the symptoms of disease in people and other living creatures, or it could be the perceived source of a disease such as sewers, rotting corpses or even unhygienic environments like a squalid dwelling or damp, moldy room.

- Infection also includes the nasty sub-group of 'Infestation'. Parasites and any nasty little blood-sucker like a mosquito or a flea. For example: Zombies.

Fear of Predators

- Fairly self-explanatory this one. Any creature that wants to kill you. The primary fear is that the predator wants to eat you or feed you to its young in some horrendous manner. But there's also a secondary fear, one of being hunted, regardless of the end result. For example: Zombies!

Fear of the Unknown

- What we don't know can't hurt us, right? For example: Invisible Zombies!!

Any of these fears can do the job for you when designing a Boss for your fictional game world. But if you really want to scare people, it's best to combine two or more. Hence the solid position that zombies still hold in popular culture.

Geiger's Aliens are another excellent example. Their skeletal biology hits the Death notes. They're a ruthless Predator. And there's also the fact that they grow like cancer within you until they're ready to burst forth from your chest cavity... that's the Infection bit.

Fear of the Unknown is the most challenging one. The first step is to hide your monster from the player for a long time. But it's also not quite as simple as that. A monster that you don't know is there is the same as a monster who isn't there at all.

The trick with Fear of the Unknown is that you must drop hints as to the identity of your monster, but nothing conclusive. Nothing that would give the player an 'Aha!' moment until they are face to face with the monster itself. Understanding should be just out of reach until it finally comes crashing down in one horrific climax.

This is why, to my mind, Alien is the scarier movie than Aliens.

> DESIGNING MY MONSTER

Here's an example of how I combined Fear of Infection and Fear of the Unknown into a monster I created for my Falconers world. It's called a "Seeder", a subspecies of a range of nature-monsters I call "Cullers".

Step 1: Decide how I want my role-player to feel when they encounter my monster.

Two words. "Creeped out!" I wanted a type of 'body snatcher' that can masquerade as a human and cause deadly conflicts within a community. But I didn't want to go with the classic 'pod people' or doppelganger way. I wanted something that would get under the reader/player's skin and crawl around in there. There's a subset of Fear of Infection, you see, and that's Fear of Infestation. That's why I looked to nature and settled on centipedes, cockroaches and maggots.

Step 2: Write a short 'biology' profile for my monster.

Species: Seeder
Function: Sew human dissent and cause intra-community conflict
Biology: Seeders are made up of a swarm of smaller creatures. Most commonly, these creatures take the form of centipedes, although other forms, such as cockroaches and maggots, occur.

The Seeder sub-creatures can act and feed independently but will come together to form a 'single body' when the Seeder needs to impersonate a human. The sub-creatures will huddle together to form a human body shape and then will excrete organic gels and resins that form a human exterior; skin, eyes, hair, nails, teeth and tongue.

The Seeder is effectively a hive mind, linking the individual brains of its sub-creatures through a combination of telepathy and pheromones. The result is an intelligence much like an AI, with the equivalent intellect of a human but completely lacking in human emotion.

Step 3: Write a 'behavior' profile to "Establish the Danger".

Then I decide the type of damage I want my monster to cause and how they inflict that damage. With Seeders, I'm not really talking about combat damage. I'm focusing on what makes this creature monstrous. How does it destroy the lives of everyday people? How does it become a source of fear and dread?

Behavior: Seeders insinuate themselves into a human community by targeting an existing member of that community. This is usually someone who is respected and has a great deal of social cache. The Seeder will then spend an extended period, from six months to a year, observing that individual in every accessible portion of their lives. It does this by mobilizing its sub-creatures, putting the target human under 24 hour surveillance. During this time, the Seeder learns the mark's language, speech patterns, routines and behaviors. It continues this observation phase until it has learned enough to mimic that individual with 100% accuracy.

Once the observation phase is complete, the Seeder will ambush the target individual and kill them. The sub-creatures will then completely consume the victim's corpse, flesh, organs and bone. They will use the resulting nutrients to excrete the exterior shell that will disguise this humanoid mass of huddled monstrosities.

With the target human gone, and the disguise in place, the Seeder will then assume their new identity and use it to sew dissent amongst the community.

Even once the human shell is in place, a Seeder will use its sub-creatures to spy on the other community members, learning their secrets. It does this by releasing individual creatures through ruptures in its shell. The ruptures are quickly repaired to maintain the integrity of the disguise. Through rumor, lies, seduction and deceit, the Seeder plays community members off against each other, raising tensions until the community turns on itself, tearing itself apart in a frenzy of fury and hatred.

Step 4: Establish a weakness. Every monster must be killable.

Like all Cullers, Seeders are most susceptible to gold, for two reasons.

1. This is the 19th Century in the gold rushes of the colonies. Gold affects every level of society.
2. Silver is already taken by werewolves.

However, shooting individual sub-creatures won't significantly damage a Culler. You have to go for the CPU, the one bug that acts as the 'hub' for the creature's hive mind. All 'thoughts' pass through this 'hub bug' so killing the bug will temporarily disrupt the hive mind. Yes, a new hub bug will be established seconds later, but until then, the Seeder is effectively paralyzed.

If the Seeder suspects that "the jig is up", it will disperse into its parts, making it practically impossible to destroy completely. The player would need to destroy the Seeder before it disperses, surrounding it with fire or smothering it in some form of pesticide.

Step 5: Google It! Ask around. Do your due diligence.

Finally, I do a series of internet searches to see if I can find anything that's like the monster I've just created. I ask my friends and colleagues in the writing and games industries if they've heard of anything like it. I search the monster's name to see what it will be associated with. If I do find something similar, I make adjustments to make sure it's not similar.

Yes, this is the not-so-fun step, but it ensures that you don't accidentally copy something that's already out there. If it's anywhere in the ballpark of something made by Disney, back away with your hands held high until you're in the relative safety of your home and drawing board.

That's right, Cthulhu is just salt and pepper calamari on the buffet table of the true 'Elder God'.

> FINALE

And there we have it. My Five Step Method for Making Monsters.

Step 1: Which fear do you want your player/reader to experience?
Step 2: Icky and gooey. The Biological profile.
Step 3: Establish the Danger. The Behavior profile.
Step 4: Monsters must Die! Establish the weakness.
Step 5: Beware the corporate Elder Gods and do your due diligence.

Happy Frankensteining!

PROCEDURAL NARRATIVE: THE FUTURE OF VIDEO GAME STORYTELLING_

Procedural Narrative is the 'hot topic' of the moment in narrative design. As more and more games become procedurally generated, there's increasing demand for storytelling strategies that are highly flexible and adaptive. Therefore, as narrative designers, we must get our heads around procedural systems and how we can use them to create satisfying story experiences.

Gone are the days when you could just slap The Hero's Journey on all and sundry. Suddenly, the player isn't just going along for the ride on a nice, smooth character arc. This isn't Booker DeWitt in Bioshock Infinite coming to terms with his past. This isn't Joel and Ellie in The Last of Us building a relationship only to have the hostile world threaten to tear it apart.

Procedural story is, to my mind, the polar opposite of linear storytelling. But before we delve into procedural narrative, we best give you a clear definition of what procedural generation in video games is.

Procedural generation: A portion of the game's content is generated by algorithms instead of being handcrafted.

For instance, a game like Enter the Gungeon has procedurally generated levels. The level designer gives the algorithm a certain number of assets to include in any given level. Several rooms, loot chests, mobs, teleporters, a shopkeeper room and a boss room. According to some nifty conditions that I won't even attempt to unpack here, the algorithm arranges these assets into a playable level.

Whenever you die in Enter the Gungeon (which is quite a lot), the algorithm rearranges the levels so that, while the assets are the same, the layout is completely different. In this way, every level feels like a fresh experience, even though the core elements are all repeated.

Yes, this is a much more economical way of generating levels than the old handcrafted method, and is a way of ensuring almost infinite replayability.

But as a writer, how do you tell a story when the story world is constantly changing? How do you write a plot about the player-character's journey to defeat the villain when both the journey and the land and never the same two times running?

Well, that's where procedural narrative comes in.

With procedural generation, the game is reacting to what the player does, not what the character is expected to do.

The Player = Protagonist

The Game = Antagonist

The Story = What happens as the Protag struggles to overcome the Antag.

There's no predictable plot here, because the Protag can succeed or fail in a myriad of ways.

Plot is replaced by Story Experience.

Okay, luckily I can now plunder one of my other books, Narrative Design for Indies, to explain what a 'Story Experience' is and how it relates to procedural generation. If you've already read ND4INdies, you might want to skip this next bit and go straight to

"What's the difference between procedural narrative and emergent narrative?" below.

> PROCEDURAL NARRATIVE = STORY EXPERIENCE

I once heard narrative design likened to theme park design. A park ride might have a story context, a must-have for any haunted house or ghost train ride, and the ticket-holder then explores that context, feeling part of that miniature world for a bit.

It's a tough thing to explain in abstract, so let's get concrete with one of my favorite ever Indie RPGs. Darkest Dungeon.

Being a rogue-like RPG, Darkest Dungeon is all about the experience of delving into Lovecraftian realms, surviving by the skin of your teeth and going completely bonkers in the process. There is no 'plot' beyond the usual fare of 'mad overreacher explores where he should not and unearths an ancient evil that then corrupts the entire place'. Sounds like a hundred games, stories and novels already, right? And it would've been no different to the rest had not the creators stopped right there and said, "Plot, shmot! Let's give the player a story-rich experience instead." I'm sure that wasn't their exact words, but the spirit of that statement permeates almost every element of Darkest Dungeon.

Darkest Dungeon wrangles its world design, glyphs and dialogue in such a way as to wrap the player in story without ever demanding that they follow any plot. As soon as a player follows a plot then their choices are limited. Darkest Dungeon's limits are mechanical, not narrative. You can pretty much engage with whichever elements you want, whenever you want, within the confines of what's possible for you at the time.

Your progress in Darkest Dungeon is defined by character levels, character health (both physical and mental) and how much of the game's hometown, The Hamlet, you've rebuilt and upgraded. In fact, the hamlet itself is as much an RPG character as the adventurers that use it as their base of operations.

For a start, the adventurers themselves are the sort of troubled types you'd find in any Lovecraftian horror.

Houndmaster:

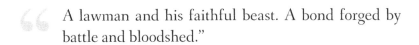 A lawman and his faithful beast. A bond forged by battle and bloodshed."

Leper:

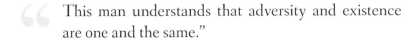 This man understands that adversity and existence are one and the same."

Antiquarian:

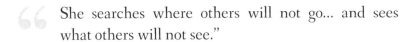 She searches where others will not go... and sees what others will not see."

That's all the backstory you get, and that's all the backstory you need in a game like Darkest Dungeon. Each adventurer is a lump of clay for the player to mould. Different varieties of clay, yes, with different properties, but with plenty of scope for the player to stamp them with personality and sculpt them with experience.

And where does all of this personality and experience come from? Well, mostly from the horrors the adventurers have to deal with in those antediluvian depths. Frightening monstrosities, eldritch curses, itchy and icky illnesses, and the ever-pervading gloom itself.

Darkest Dungeon needs no character arcs nor ticking plot devices. It has game mechanics! Each adventurer has a Stress counter. When that stress counter rises too high, the adventurer in question 'cracks' and develops some rather peculiar psychological maladies. Selfishness, masochism, hopelessness, irrationality and paranoia... this list of afflictions goes on.

The result? The adventurers start to behave differently during combat. A 'masochist' will race to the front of the party of their own volition so they can invite the most damage upon themselves. An adventurer who is feeling 'hopeless' may skip their combat turn. A 'fearful' adventurer will shift themselves to the back of the pack whilst ranting in such a terrified manner that it raises everyone else's stress counts. An 'abusive' adventurer will cast aspersions on his party-mates, resulting in ever increased stress counts.

In a nutshell, or nutcase in this instance, each character's story context is expressed through mechanics and succinct text bubbles. No expensive voice over (apart from that wonderfully creepy narrator), no plot to adhere too, and yet the group dynamics are as clear and complex an expression as one might find in a soap opera.

Rogue-like RPGs are renowned for their procedurally generated environments and MOB encounters. Darkest Dungeon is renowned for its procedurally generated story.

> PROCEDURAL NARRATIVES REQUIRE NONLINEAR THINKING

But how do you 'write' for something like that?

For a start, you switch off all the lights in your plot brain except for that one desk lamp at the workstation called Department of Cause and Effect. Then you get down to the business of writing tiny scripts, sometimes just one line, that capture specific moments of cause and effect in your game.

For instance, let's look at some PC Area Dialogues from Path of Exile, the lines that a selected player-character will say the first time they enter a new area or perhaps when they kill a Unique Mob or Boss within that area.

The Witch

Killing Hillock:

> Too stupid to know he was dead already.

Entering Fellshrine:

> Looks like the faithful have gone to that 'better place' of theirs.

Killing Fidelitas:

> What a pretty creation!

Entering Act 3, City of Sarn:

> A big, dead city. My favorite.

Entering Sewers:

> Humanity is gone yet the stink remains.

Entering the Marketplace:

> Screams upon screams, as soft as the faintest whisper.

Entering Catacombs:

The 'worthy' like to bury their secrets deep.

Entering Ebony Barracks:

 Damnation has no wrath like a witch scorned.

These lines are spread out right across Path of Exile, but each is a piece of the jigsaw puzzle that is the Witch's character. We learn about her as a 'person' only when she reacts to elements in the game world, and at these points we also get the chance to add a little more meaning to the environment. We can include scents and stenches that can't otherwise be expressed. We can add insights into cultures that would otherwise have to be explained through story glyphs.

 Damnation has no wrath like a witch scorned."

This is a play on the commonly heard phrase, "Hell hath no fury like a woman scorned." So there's a 'feminine vengeance' energy to it. And it's directed at the Templar baddies who, as patriarchal religious zealots, tend to send witches into 'damnation' upon a burning pyre. Yes, a right lovely bunch, the Templar of Oriath. A 'cross' between Bible Belt evangelists and the Spanish Inquisition.

 The 'worthy' like to bury their secrets deep."

Yes, another potshot at devout Templar hypocrisy.

By the end of developing Act 5 of Path of Exile, each player-character had almost one hundred lines of dialogue, tailored as character-informing reactions to the environments and monsters that inhabit them. There are seven PCs to choose from, so we had roughly seven hundred lines.

That's a lot of tiny little pieces of narrative confetti, but when added together throughout the course of the game, they coagulate into seven fully formed characters, each with a unique perspective on their journey through Wraeclast and beyond.

To create a one-hundred-line reaction script like that, we can look at each environment, one by one, and write each line as we go along. It's the same with the Boss-kill dialogues and any other incidentals, like running out of Mana or having a full inventory. Every line is drawn from the context in which it will be said.

Templar PC

 I'm no beast of burden."

With Path of Exile, we can show some character development because there's a rough order to the areas that can be entered, and to the bosses that can be slain. If the player progresses through the game 'as expected' then it's possible to even create a plot. But 'expected' is not the same as 'predictable' when it comes to player behavior. Yes, you can exhaustively playtest and peer like a soothsayer into the entrails of your back end stats, but if there's any freedom in your game then players will do things in whatever order is more convenient and enjoyable to them.

Some bosses can be avoided rather than slain. Some side areas might not be entered until the player has completed all the main ones. Quest items might be carried around for several Acts before being handed onto the appropriate NPC.

Every line has to make sense in isolation while also fitting together into a whole that feels right for our PC's personality. And to do this, we snap our neatly linear ruler in twain and wrap the halves upon our desk like drumsticks as we focus on what's *really* important.

> PROCEDURAL NARRATIVE NEEDS THEME AND TONE

The Duelist

Waking up on the beach:

" Sand and the faint aroma of death. I think I've found my new arena.

Killing Hillock:

" Twice as big, twice as dead.

Entering the Southern Forest:

" Good to feel the sun on my face again.

Entering the (Fellshrine) Crypt:

" Smells of dust and dead devotions.

Killing Fidelitas:

" I'm not sure if I've just killed a man or squished a bug.

Entering the City of Sarn:

" This must have been a truly glorious city in its day.

Theme: Glory. An ongoing obsession with achieving and maintaining self-glorification.

Tone: Quick-witted and light-hearted. Charming and geared towards amusing others.

Once you know the Theme and Tone, you pretty much know how the Duelist will react in any situation. He glorifies the stuff he likes and makes jokes about the stuff he dislikes. And as he gradually realizes the brutality he is inflicting in his quest for glory, and feels the emptiness of glory's attainment, the glorification becomes less enthusiastic and the jokes a little darker.

The Duelist gradually learns that Wraeclast is not just a giant arena laid out for his own glorification. That's his story, and the player finds that out by simply experiencing their exile in all of its gory glory.

WHAT'S THE DIFFERENCE BETWEEN PROCEDURAL NARRATIVE AND EMERGENT NARRATIVE?_

These are my working definitions for Procedural and Emergent, what I use when creating game narratives for my clients.

There's a ton of waffle out there about procedural narrative and emergent narrative, so I will get straight to the point. But remember, I'm not an academic. I'm a working professional who is industriously oblivious of the canon surrounding the terms 'procedural' and 'emergent'.

I defined procedural narrative as a narrative design strategy. Basically, you create a bunch of little narrative bites, from tomes and flavor texts to dialogues and visual motifs. Then you scatter them across your game so the player can find them in any order.

As mentioned in the previous chapter, procedurally generated games have a randomized element to them where the game world forms in different ways with each playthrough. Darkest Dungeon is an excellent example of this. Dozens of room types, monsters, loot and nasty experiences shuffled around so that every dungeon delve offers a different combination.

Story elements become one of the many game assets that get shuffled about. So when designing these elements I make sure that they are both self-contained, like a poem, and connected to the larger theme, like a poetry collection.

Emergent narrative is the ultimate goal of all this micro-design and shuffling about malarkey. For a single-player gamer (like me), the narrative emerges as I explore the game and encounter all of these story fragments. Naturally, my experience and understanding of that story will differ from another player who encounters those story fragments in a different order and under different circumstances.

It's all about juxtaposition. For instance...

 Every story has an ending."

Imagine this line in the setting of a labyrinth you're trying to escape. Now imagine it on a brightly lit mountain meadow after you've just tumbled out of that labyrinth. Now imagine it while you're surrounded by giant spiders or an army of the undead.

How the player feels in that moment, and how that emotion informs their interpretation of the story fragment... that is emergent narrative.

Procedural narrative is the design strategy, emergent narrative is the outcome, the player's experience.

To my mind, emergent narrative goes one step further. Now that the most popular games in the world are generally multi-player, narrative interpretation is taken into the forums and chat rooms. A player's experience of a procedural narrative is shared and compared with others so that deeper understanding is gained of the game's story themes. The experience is no longer singular. It becomes a discourse, and therefore 'agreed upon interpretations' emerge out of the games procedural narrative.

So let me recap.

Procedural Narrative: A design technique where a game's story comprises many fragments that can be collected, experienced and interpreted in many orders and ways.

Emergent Narrative: The result of that collection and interpretation process. It's the individual player's experience of a narrative alphabet soup, and it's the gaming collective's efforts to turn the alphabet soup into a linear narrative that can be summarized and agreed upon.

Procedural is how the game story is made.
Emergent is the story experience the gamer takes home.

> FINAL THOUGHT ON EMERGENT NARRATIVE

Yes, it's arguable that emergent narrative is enough all by itself. You don't need a procedural narrative design because emergent storytelling fills in the gaps. This is very much the case with a game like Rimworld where the player community actively shares and compares each other's Rimworld experiences in a kind of 'campfire storytelling' way.

I don't think it matters whether the storytelling is shared or private. It's still emergent. But heck, as soon as we turned clothes pegs into soldiers as kids, we were making emergent narrative. Rimworld is more intentional, as in it's deliberately provoking emergent narrative, but I personally crave something more complete.

I want a game that will allow me to generate a narrative on the fly and deliver it in a polished, satisfying way.

I don't ask for much, eh.

WHERE (I THINK) PROCEDURAL NARRATIVE NEEDS TO GO NEXT_

I played Rimworld because it was touted as a wonder of procedural narrative, one of the few games to take the approach seriously and do it well. I returned from that raw frontier with some very mixed feelings indeed.

> STORY ENGINE OR PLOT ENGINE?

Rimworld is remarkably good at generating plot on the fly. You have your three little spacewreck survivors who you set to work, salvaging supplies, building themselves a home, planting crops and so on. Basic town builder stuff.

But Rimworld goes much deeper than your average town builder. Each survivor has a set of basic Needs, like the need for an aesthetically pleasing home, the need to feel like a civilized human being who eats at a table. The need for recreation, the need for comfortable clothing.

If you don't supply those needs within your settlement, those lacking elements can affect the physical and mental health of your survivors.

For instance, no one enjoys seeing a rotting human body. At least not in Rimworld. Raiders of various kinds will turn up and try to attack the settlement. If your survivors manage to kill them, then you need to dig graves for the resulting corpses or your people will become troubled by the sight and smell of rotting cadavers. There are no magically dissolving bodies in Rimworld.

Once affected too deeply by their consternations, your survivors will start confining themselves to bed, going for long contemplative walks, or may just lie down somewhere and stare at the sky. On the emotional level, characters can eventually 'break'. They can go mad.

Then there are the environmental factors that make for any good survival story. Wild animal attacks. Heat waves and cold snaps. The constant struggle for food.

A friend and fellow game developer told me how, after a particularly harsh winter, his survivors were forced to eat each other. A wife ended up eating her husband. This is great 'human vs wilderness' stuff!

In theory.

I say this because, while Rimworld's mechanics do a wonderful job of procedurally generating the narrative of harsh life on a frontier world, it doesn't do a very good job of presenting that narrative.

The art style is rudimentary. Necessarily so because it's been made by a tiny Indie team. But with that comes the feeling that you're observing ants in an ant farm rather than people in a struggling colony.

The physical and emotional well-being of your characters are presented as statistics and basic statements.

-3 for not sitting at a table to eat a meal.
-5 for lacking any form of recreation.
Shoulder wound.

Vegetarian.

The narrative is coldly summarized in neat little stat boxes. It's like reading the plot summary of a Shakespeare play rather than experiencing a live production. It's all there in the summary, but it has the emotional potency of a tax form.

Many will disagree with me on this point. Rimworld has many fans who become deeply invested in their characters. And much of the pleasure of Rimworld seems to come from sharing your Rimworld experience with others.

"My botanist had to go cannibal on her sculptor husband!"

This is where procedural narrative becomes emergent narrative. The pleasure is not so much in the original telling of the story by the game. It comes from the retelling to other players.

Rimworld delivers a unique narrative with every playthrough. No two play experiences are alike. Therefore, Rimworld experiences are great for sharing around a virtual campfire because your story will always be fresh to your listeners.

But 'here's the rub', going back to my Shakespeare analogy. Rimworld's creator, Tynan Sylvester, claims that his game is a 'story generator'. I think that's misleading, but it's also just another example of the general misunderstandings around the definitions of narrative, story and plot. I would call Rimworld a plot generator. It would be a brilliant plot outlining tool.

Survivors build settlement.

Survivors run out of food during winter.

Survivors eat each other.

This happens then this happens then this happens. That's plot. Story is how those plot points are expressed.

> WHERE PROCEDURAL NARRATIVE MEETS STORYTELLING

For examples of how a procedural narrative can be expressed as a powerful story, I need go no further than Sunless Sea and Darkest Dungeon. While not as mechanically rich as Rimworld, both games do a much better job of expressing a procedurally generated narrative as an emotionally effective story.

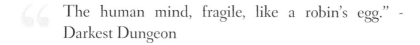

The human mind, fragile, like a robin's egg." - Darkest Dungeon

This is one of the DD narrator's lines when one of your adventurers cracks under pressure and ends up with a mental disorder.

Even the aged oak will fall to the tempest's winds." - Darkest Dungeon

Through a combination of beautifully written dialogue, comic-style still images and evocative voice over, Darkest Dungeon captures the moment of a character's mental distress far more powerfully than...

Mental State: Psychotic wandering" - Rimworld

With Sunless Sea, these dark and dramatic moments are expressed through text alone. However, the way these moments are written provides a wonderful sense of bleak tragedy.

Day by day, you all grow weaker. Each sip of fresh water is carefully rationed. Zailors squabble over scraps of leather. Each morning, bodies are found stiff and cold." - Sunless Sea

Feast on their remains - You are past the edge of desperation. They have died: you will live." - Sunless Sea

In Rimworld, Darkest Dungeon and Sunless Sea, "shit happens". A nasty turn of events can come from your own poor decision making or completely out of the blue. Just like in life.

But there's a big difference between procedural narrative and story. The plot that's generated by the systems in these games, to me, is nothing without the effective expression of that plot in emotional terms. Stat boxes and rudimentary graphics simply don't carry the emotional gravitas of well-written prose, striking illustrations, and evocative voice over.

The plot must be shown to have meaning for the characters involved in that plot. And the expression of that meaning must pluck at the heartstrings.

> PROCEDURAL NARRATIVE NEEDS POWERFUL FICTION

While stats and states can stir the soul for some, most players need their storytelling to be more traditional, a little closer to what they expect from film, television, books and AAA video games like Assassin's Creed, God of War and The Last of Us.

Rather than reading a plot summary of MacBeth, we need to experience the live performance.

A plot point can be generated by a procedural system, but that plot point still needs to be expressed as a story, otherwise it remains a fact rather than an experience.

Not that you need to be AAA to tell game stories that audiences will love. Far from it! Indie games, like Darkest Dungeon and Sunless Sea, prove that compelling stories can be expressed through a combination of procedural narrative and effective storytelling.

To me, this is where procedural narrative needs to go next. The systems are in place. Now storytellers need to step in and turn those procedurally generated facts into powerfully expressed fictions.

The ghost must be inserted into the machine.

EPILOGUE_

> GETTING YOUR HEAD IN THE GAME(S)

Have I changed your mind about this whole narrative design malarkey? Have I reinforced a few thoughts you already had about this crazy ND business? Have I put you off entirely?

Hopefully, the former two and not the latter.

The thing is, the mindset required for narrative design is so very different from any other writing mindset I've encountered. And I've tried most of them for myself.

A Bit of Everything

I've written short stories, novels, non-fiction books and poetry. I've written storylines and scripts for television, film, comics, radio and theatre.

When I started in games, I rather cockily thought the transition would be a breeze. I had a Masters in Scriptwriting and four years of professional television writing under my belt. Not to mention all the other types of writing I'd done off my own bat.

Oh, how wrong could I be?

With linear forms of storytelling, it's all about the structure.

Start, middle and end. Where's your inciting incident, your darkest moment, your climax and your satisfying finish?

I'm simplifying, I know. There are many, many examples of novels, TV shows and films that don't follow that tried and true 'Hero's Journey'. But in saying that, there are so many that do.

Scratch the surface of the top selling films of all time and you'll find Joseph Campbell peeking up at you through the special effects.

But with games, there's no such underlying story structure. No 'industry standard' formula like the Hero's Journey. For instance, look at this Wikipedia list of the best-selling games of all time (so far).

- Minecraft
- Tetris
- Grand Theft Auto V
- Wii Sports
- PlayerUnknown's Battlegrounds
- Super Mario Bros
- Pokémon Red/Green/Blue/Yellow
- Wii Fit and Wii Fit Plus
- Mario Kart Wii
- Wii Sports Resort
- Mario Kart 8
- New Super Mario Bros
- The Elder Scrolls V: Skyrim
- Diablo III and Reaper of Souls
- Pokémon Gold/Silver/Crystal
- Duck Hunt
- Wii Play
- Grand Theft Auto: San Andreas
- Terraria
- Call of Duty: Modern Warfare

- Red Dead Redemption 2
- Call of Duty: Black Ops
- Grand Theft Auto IV
- Pokémon Sun/Moon/Ultra Sun/Ultra Moon
- Pokémon Diamond/Pearl/Platinum
- Call of Duty: Black Ops II
- FIFA 18
- Kinect Adventures!
- Sonic the Hedgehog
- Nintendogs
- Mario Kart DS
- Call of Duty: Modern Warfare
- Pokémon Ruby/Sapphire/Emerald
- Borderlands 2
- Super Mario World
- Frogger
- Grand Theft Auto: Vice City
- Lemmings
- The Witcher 3: Wild Hunt
- Brain Age
- Super Mario Bros. 3
- Call of Duty: Ghosts
- Mario Kart 7
- Super Mario Land
- The Legend of Zelda: Breath of the Wild
- Super Smash Bros. Ultimate
- Grand Theft Auto III
- The Last of Us
- Super Mario Odyssey

With the notable exception of Tetris, the above games all needed at least some narrative design input. For the older games, pre-2000, there probably wasn't a writer on board. It was most likely the game designers doing the story stuff. But post-2000? All those encouraging things the yoga instructor says to you in Wii Fit? Yes, a writer came up with those lines.

At the other end of the spectrum you have massive narrative undertakings like The Last of Us, a classic example of the Hero's Journey in action. But then you have Witcher 3 which has a Hero's Journey as its main plot, but then offers an entire world of jigsawing storytelling for players looking for exploration and general RPG immersion.

So if there's no set role, no prescribed skill set for writers in the games industry, how does a narrative designer find their way into gainful employment?

Start by playing to your strengths. Perhaps it's scriptwriting? Perhaps it's flavor text? Perhaps it's narrative strategy? Perhaps it's environmental storytelling?

We can't be good at everything. We're only human.

And it's hard to know what your strengths even are when you're starting out, but if you have any inkling that you might be stronger in one area than another, go find the developers who need that particular strength, play their games, and maybe even approach them for work.

Down the track though, as you're pushing to go full time as a narrative designer, it'll pay to diversify.

Because here's what I think is the biggest mindset shift when it comes to forging a sustainable career as a narrative designer.

Constant upskilling.

You have to be prepared to tackle a whole new storytelling paradigm on every new game writing gig.

This is honestly how I've survived this last ten years as a narrative designer. I've kept my scope wide open so I can take on just about any type of gig that's going.

I might do narrative strategy for a rogue-like space exploration game one day, flavor text for a collectable card game the next day, and mission dialogue for a cute fish-themed town builder over the weekend. In fact, on any given workday, I might do all three things, and some character design for a 2D platformer on the side. Or some prose for a corporate interactive fiction aimed at making job interviews more engaging.

I'm speaking from the freelancer's perspective here. I can't really say what goes on in a staff writer's day because I've never been one. If you're a staff scriptwriter for a Bioware game, you may well just write dialogue scripts all day every day. But those gigs are few. For the rest of us, we need to piece together a career out of lots of different games. And that means being versatile.

There's another reason for fast learning and versatility too.

> TECHNOLOGY

Games, more than any other form of storytelling, are driven by technology. And as we all know, nothing these days changes faster than technology. Mobile gaming was barely even a thing prior to 2007. Only thirteen years ago. Now look at it. Estimated to be worth $68.5 billion at the end of 2019.

But will mobile gaming still be around in another thirteen years? Will it even be recognizable in five years' time if game streaming and phone / controller combos take off? We just don't know.

All we know is that change is inevitable, and it's happening all the time now.

As new technology arises, the next wave being AR and VR, narrative design techniques have to change to make the most of these new ways of experiencing story.

Yes, as a narrative designer, you need to be a tech lover. Or a tech tolerator, at the very least. If you find yourself already scratching your head, wondering what the point is of all these newfangled inventions, you might want to consider another career.

But if you're determined, then trust in the fact that your brain is amazing.

Why?

Neuroplasticity.

The constantly shifting realities of the games industry may feel overwhelming at first, but it's astounding how quickly your brain can adjust. With concentration and patience, your mindset will develop beyond the anxiety and the headaches. The more you challenge them, the deeper and more sophisticated your neural networks will become.

Your narrative designer's mindset will become literally hard wired into your wetware.

Keep playing.

Keep writing.

Keep learning.

The games industry needs you.

I'm serious.

It really does.

⊏▭⊐

NEXT STEP_

If you love video games, sci-fi and fantasy, join my Lorekeeper group. Enjoy a fortnightly newsletter all about gamethink and the odd bit of gamelit.

https://www.edmcrae.com/lorekeepers

ABOUT THE AUTHOR_

Edwin McRae has been a screenwriter and narrative designer for over 13 years now. After four years of writing for television, he started with Grinding Gear Games in 2010. He became lead writer on the creative team that took their online ARPG, Path of Exile, from 80,000 players to 20 million players and a 100 million dollar buyout from Tencent. Over the past decade he's worked with numerous Indie game developers, helping them turn their ideas into stories that players can experience and enjoy.

Website: www.edmcrae.com
Facebook: www.facebook.com/edwinmcraewriter
Discord: https://discord.gg/gUxD9gw

ALSO BY EDWIN MCRAE_

Narrative Design for Indies: Getting Started

Guardian Māia

The Falconers: Moonlight

Warlock: Reign of Blood

Executioner: Reign of Blood

Skulls of Atlantis

Made in the USA
Monee, IL
01 May 2022